P9-DMX-854

EATING WITH PETER

EATING WITH PETER

A Gastronomic Journey

Stories and Recipes

SUSAN BUCKLEY

Illustrations by Dana Catharine

Arcade Publishing • New York

First Edition

Arcade Publishing books may be purchased in bulk at special discounts for sales promotion, corporate gifts, fund-raising, or educational purposes. Special editions can also be created to specifications. For details, contact the Special Sales Department, Arcade Publishing, 307 West 36th Street, 11th Floor, New York, NY 10018 or arcade@skyhorsepublishing.com.

Arcade Publishing® is a registered trademark of Skyhorse Publishing, Inc.®, a Delaware corporation.

Visit our website at www.arcadepub.com.

10 9 8 7 6 5 4 3 2 1

Names: Buckley, Susan Washburn, author.
Title: Eating with Peter : a gastronomic journey : stories & recipes / by Susan Buckley ; illustrations by Dana Catharine.
Description: New York : Arcade Publishing, [2018] | Includes bibliographical references and index.
Identifiers: LCCN 2017052457 (print) | LCCN 2017056339 (ebook) | ISBN 9781628728767 (ebook) | ISBN 9781628728750 (hardcover : alk. paper)
Subjects: LCSH: Gastronomy. | Buckley, Susan Washburn--Travel. | Buckley, Susan Washburn--Family. | Authors--United States--Biography. | International cooking. | LCGFT: Cookbooks.
Classification: LCC TX631 (ebook) | LCC TX631 .B83 2018 (print) | DDC 641.01/3--dc23
LC record available at https://lccn.loc.gov/2017052457

Cover design by Brian Peterson

Printed in China

Grateful acknowledgment is made for the following excerpts:
pp. 59–61 from *les recettes originales de Jean et Pierre Troisgros, Cuisiniers à Roanne* (Editions Robert Laffont, © 1977)

p. 70 from *Feasts for All Seasons* by Roy Andries de Groot (Penguin Random House © 1966)

For Peter, of course

And for David, Annabel, and Michael,
who had to put up with us

Contents

Introduction

There are many people like other people, but there was no one like Peter Buckley.

—Simon Michael Bessie, publisher

Being married to Peter Buckley was not always easy—living with larger-than-life personalities seldom is—but it was *never* boring. After Peter departed this mortal coil in 1997, our eye doctor mused one day: "I miss Mr. Buckley," he said. "You know, when he came into the office, it was like being at a play. You never knew what was going to happen next!"

For twenty-five years I shared my life with this fascinating, lovable, brilliant, funny, sweet, outsized, outspoken, outrageous, and sometimes impossible man. And for all of those years, food played a big role—finding it, cooking it, eating it, reading about it, writing about it, traveling for it.

As in all lives and all marriages, there were good times and hard times. This book is about the good times, when eating with Peter was always an adventure.

EATING WITH PETER

IN THE BEGINNING

Once, as a child, I made the startling announcement that I wanted to be either a foreign correspondent or a missionary when I grew up. Aspirations to be a glamorous journalist made perfect sense, but a missionary? Why on earth would I have wanted to be a missionary? Clearly, travel was the operative theme.

Travel! In the world I inhabited in the 1950s, going to Europe for the summer was a new and enticing opportunity. Every summer my mother's teacher friends in New Jersey took off to explore Western Europe. But my mother and I were committed to going back to the small town in Louisiana where we'd both grown up. That had its own deep appeal, but it wasn't the romantic world I envisioned as a teenager. An omnivorous reader, I wanted to be an archeologist uncovering Mayan ruins or Schliemann at Troy. By the time I was in college, I wanted to go to Paris in the twenties, to Saint Petersburg and the court of Nicolas and Alexandra, to Venice with Henry James.

In the summer of 1963, a newly minted Middlebury graduate, I went to Europe at last. Having grown up in Southwest Louisiana, where delicious food was central to life, I was a good eater, but food was not my holy grail on that trip. It was all about the past. I'd spent four years reading the canon of English literature and studying European history. It was Tennyson, not truffles, that I was after.

Before I finally took off, however, my mother insisted that I learn how to do *something* with my new degree in English literature. So, she enrolled me in the Radcliffe Summer Secretarial course, designed to give young ladies the skills they would need (typing, something arcane called "speed writing," and general office skills that would make up for our majoring in English, art history, and other unemployable subjects). It is hard to imagine now that Radcliffe would have thought it appropriate to teach a few hundred girls how to type faster so they could get jobs, but that was the world of 1963—just before it was turned on its ear. It might have been 1963, but "the Sixties" hadn't started yet in my universe.

At last, on a late summer day, I flew to Europe on an eighteen-hour, transatlantic flight on Icelandic Airlines, the successor to the student ships of the past. Excited but nervous, I landed in Luxembourg (Icelandic's only European destination), on my way to Paris to meet three friends who had been traveling all summer. (Their mothers did *not* make them go to Radcliffe.) In short order, I was installed in a European hotel from another century, rococo and very grand.

I am sure I didn't wear a hat to dinner but I'll bet I carried gloves. After making my way to the enormous dining room, which resembled something out of *The Merry Widow*, I soon found myself faced with a waiter in formal dress, looking like no other waiter I had ever encountered—and speaking French, a language I yearned to speak but was appallingly unable to even after years of high school and college classes. I smiled shyly and looked down at the menu. Quickly I spotted the word "entrée." Ah, the main course, I thought, like the good American that I am. I figured out the listing for smoked trout and ordered that. Did I not want something more, the waiter inquired? "*Non, merci*," I answered, trying to look very confident. Shortly, the bemused man arrived with a very small piece of smoked trout on a very large plate.

Not until later would I realize that "entrée" in French meant your entrance to the meal, what I would have called an appetizer. I was far too proud to admit my mistake, however. Given the years of eating with Peter that were to come—the meals savored at farmhouse tables and three-star restaurants, the markets and kitchens and menus explored—my very first meal in Europe was ironically unsatisfying.

The next morning, still hungry, I took the train to Paris, where Michele and Charlotte and Penny swept me up in the end of their summer-long trip. As we careened around in our tiny Volkswagen Beetle, there it was—Paris, the "real live, truly Paris." Paris, my dream of what Europe was supposed to look and feel like. En route to a hotel where our room was almost out of our budget—five dollars a day just for the room at a time when *Europe on $5 a Day* was the guide for all young travelers!—I kept up a steady stream of squeals and sighs, for Paris looked *just* the way Paris had looked in my dreams. It was gray and beautiful and of course unlike anything I had ever experienced before, with its wide boulevards and Belle Époque buildings. Did I really see a man on a bike with a baguette under his arm, or was I just imagining that Doisneau photograph? And all of those small children speaking French so skillfully! How *did* they do it?

For the next three months I made the 1960s version of the college girl's Grand Tour—sometimes with friends and sometimes alone. I made some valiant efforts to find a job and stay, but I wasn't quite brave enough to take the chances that would have required. It would be ten years before I returned to Europe with Peter, but the romance of that first trip has stayed in my heart forever. It was all a dream to me. I imagined myself cavorting with Hemingway and Fitzgerald or walking into Forster's room with a view. A deeply committed novel reader since childhood, I had long years of practice in inhabiting other worlds. And here were worlds that I wanted to be part of—even if only in my imagination. It was an experience that changed my life, for it prepared the way for the seduction of eating with Peter.

By November, Northern Europe had turned cold and rainy, and I was eager to get home to "real life as a grown-up." What was being grown-up to my naïve twenty-two-year-old self? Moving to Manhattan, getting a job in publishing, and meeting the man of my dreams—as simple as that (which, of course, turned out not to be simple at all). It may have been 1963, but I was a child of the fifties. Looking back at it all now, I am amazed that I wasn't more calculating in deciding how to shape my life. Shouldn't I have followed the advice of the English professor who wanted me to go to graduate school? Shouldn't I have followed my dream of being a newspaper reporter, which in those days meant working in Peoria for ten years before you could get a job as a copy girl at any of New York's six or seven daily papers?

But Manhattan was the place I wanted to be, just like those lucky college interns at *Seventeen Magazine* whom I'd envied for years. With a speed unimaginable today, I found an apartment on the Upper East Side with a beloved cousin, also fresh out of college, and a job as an editorial secretary at a venerable publisher, Holt, Rinehart & Winston (surely that speed writing certificate was the key, Radcliffe would have claimed, but in reality it was all about the contacts of a family friend).

The Feminine Mystique came out that year, and the

rumblings of something called "the Women's Movement" were beginning. "Consciousness raising" groups were being formed. But I was a funny combination of already-raised consciousness and not. My Louisiana grandmother had graduated from Northwestern University in 1902, determined to have a career as an elocutionist. And she did. My mother had a graduate degree from Columbia University and had worked since I was five. So professional women were part of my DNA. On the other hand, that "child of the fifties" mentality made me not notice for many months that young women were hired as editorial secretaries and their male counterparts were hired as editorial assistants, one rung higher. I was so excited to have a job at a Madison Avenue publishing company that—to a degree that shocks me now—equality was not on my radar.

With my salary of eighty dollars a week and a measly two weeks of vacation a year, another trip to Europe was not in my immediate future, but dreams were. Just about the time I stepped onto the stage of Manhattan, Scribner published Hemingway's posthumous memoir, *A Moveable Feast*. Today, it's hard to imagine the impact of *A Moveable Feast* on impressionable young dreamers like me in 1964. The memoir really was a work of fiction, but it pulled you into what purported to be the paradigm of a Bohemian life in Paris in the twenties. I know a lot more about Ernest Hemingway now, a lot more about what really was going on in his early Paris years. But I took him at his word in 1964—and what romantic words they were. Hemingway is out of fashion these days, but then he still personified a time when young Americans from the "New World" were discovering the "Old World"—sipping absinthe at the Select, sitting at the knee of Gertrude Stein, carousing with bullfighters in Pamplona, and later dying for a cause on a Spanish hillside.

I was not alone in my dreams of Paris in the twenties, either. My good friend Molly couldn't wait to tell me about her interview for a job at Scribner. Waiting in the reception room, she overheard one editor calling out to another: "Jim, just when is Zelda's birthday?" For us, those Paris days seemed somehow touchable, a place and time we could transport ourselves back to. When I saw Woody Allen's *Midnight in Paris*, almost fifty years later, I knew just what it was all about.

Although I was deep into *A Moveable Feast,* my young single life in Manhattan was far more prosaic. Then one day as I sat typing away, who filled up my office door but a handsome bear of a man, six foot four, with a booming voice and an alluring reputation. I had seen him striding down the corridors of Holt, Rinehart & Winston. "That's Peter Buckley," I was told. "He was a friend of Ernest Hemingway." A writer and photographer, Peter had just returned after months traveling from Mexico to the tip of South America, building a photo collection for Holt's foreign language department. Now he was coming to see my boss, who wanted him to create something radical: a truly integrated textbook series, based on photographs of real kids in New York City (it's hard to believe now, but in those days all textbooks were lily white). For the next five years, Peter became a fixture of the Holt School Department, appearing in the office like a gruff but endearing Pied Piper, trailed by the fascinated children whose stories he was telling in the Holt Urban Social Studies series.

At the start of all this, Peter was married, and I was on again/off again in love with Mike Swanson, the boyfriend du jour. My friends called him "Mr. Swansong," because we were always breaking up. For a few years Peter was a fascinating character, viewed from afar. Then we became friends when I began working on his books. By this time, I was a budding young editor, thrilled to have my very first real author. Looking back, I realize that Peter—fifteen years older than I—was gently amused by my youthful enthusiasm, but in fact let me edit very little. He took to calling me Trixie, for "editrix." At first I was a little shy and more than a little overwhelmed. But Peter, underneath that sophisticated veneer, was a generous soul who swept any willing participants into his adventures. As I would come to learn, enjoying life was at the core of how he structured everything he did. Soon he'd created a whole scenario around the children and the school on which the Urban series centered. He was serving lunch in the school cafeteria, where the children called him Mr. Peanut Butter. He was finding schools and jobs for the families he featured in his books.

When A. E. Hotchner's book *Papa Hemingway* came out around this time, there was much buzzing about its photos and anecdotes of Peter and Ernest and the exotic world of Spanish bullfighting, which Peter had been part of in the 1950s. Those were the days when Peter would come into the office to talk to me, his then editor, after which he would swoop up all of the BYGs in the department to go to the Russian Tea Room or the Oak Room bar or some other place that seemed totally foreign and glamorous (the BYGs were the "bright young girls" as the older staff members wryly called us). Peter would romance us all with stories about the old days when he hung out at the Russian Tea Room with his friends in the ballet world or when he met Sinclair Lewis at the Oak Room bar.

The more I worked with Peter, the closer friends we became. Unpredictably, I—always too worried about what other people think of me—was drawn to this larger-than-life character who marched to his own drummer more than anyone I'd ever known, who was so intensely curious about everything and everyone, who could be totally outrageous but also generous and kind. Was it because he was so smart? An intellectual who was an even more voracious reader than I was? A writer as I'd always dreamt of being? Or was it because he was funny and playful and turned everything into an adventure?

Then of course there was that whole backstory. Peter took for granted a world and a life that were both foreign and attractive to me, dreamer of Parisian dreams. Taken to Europe as an infant by his mother, Elinor (who decided, for reasons she took to the grave, that she did not want to be married to his father any longer), Peter grew up in Paris, Rome, London, Geneva, and Vienna. With a French governess and an array of steamer trunks, Elinor and Peter traipsed from one European capital to another between 1926 to 1938, until the threat of war forced them to return to New York. An elegant and intellectual woman, Elinor was part of the whole "Paris in the twenties" world. It was through her friendship with Ernest Hemingway, his first wife, Hadley, and their son Jack—called "Bumby"—that Peter first knew Ernest. While Elinor occupied herself with everything from the League of Nations to an affair with an Italian count, Peter went to the French Lycée, where if you were on page ten in Paris on Monday, you were on page eleven in Geneva on Tuesday—schooling designed for diplomats and peripatetic souls like Elinor Buckley, who moved their children without great thought for the consequences. One consequence for Peter was that he was bilingual in French and English, more French than American in his manners and his proclivities.

By the time I met him, Peter had been in World War II, plucked out of his first year at Princeton when he turned eighteen in September of 1943. He used to say the only time his parents cooperated after his conception was when they pulled many strings to get him out of the infantry and into counterintelligence school. After spending the rest of the war "at home" in France, catching escaping Nazis, he came back to the United States, graduated from Princeton, and returned to France to get a PhD at the Sorbonne under the great philosopher Gaston Bachelard. Given the horrors of World War II, his thesis topic was to be "The Auto-Destructive Instincts of Man." After a year or so, however, he decided that everything to be said on this heavy topic had been said—both in writing and in two world wars. *Ça suffit*, he decided. So being Peter, he did two things: first, without agonizing, he decided to give up the musty, fusty philosophy classes at the Sorbonne, and then he went to Spain to follow the bullfights, in the process of which, he renewed the friendship with Hemingway begun in his childhood, became a filmmaker, and then became the writer and photographer he would be for the rest of his life.

At first, I didn't realize how drawn to Peter I was. Once, in an on-again moment with Mr. Swansong, I took him to Peter's apartment. Peter was shooting photographs for the filmstrips to go along with the Holt Urban series, and Mike and I were to play the parents of the children in the scenario. It was fun to see Peter at home and to meet David, Annabel, and Michael, his rambunctious young children, who were cavorting around the house dancing to the Beatles' latest album, *Yellow Submarine.* But when we left, Mike was clearly angry. "What in the world is the matter?" I asked. "Why aren't you with me like you are with that Peter Buckley?" he retorted bitterly. I was completely startled, but when I brooded over what Mike had said, I realized that he was right; by this time, I was totally myself with Peter, and I was not with him.

By 1970, Peter was divorced and setting up a new apartment for himself and the children, who divided their time between their mother's and their father's abodes. Like everything else about Peter, the new apartment was bold and colorful and European. There were French bowls and Italian plates, Danish utensils and Marimekko shades, walls covered with tapestries and African masks and Goya etchings and endless shelves of books.

It was at this point that Peter became a cook. I'm not sure who cooked in the East 84th Street apartment he'd lived in before, but the new apartment—on East 83rd Street—quickly became a cook's home. Not only were there all of those beautiful plates and bowls, but there were copper pans Elinor had brought back from France in the thirties and French cookbooks and a big wooden spoon from Spain for serving paella. There were gallons of fabulous olive oil and cases of wine (I, who was just emerging from the world of too-sweet Mateus in those funny bottles, found the idea of buying wine by the case ultra-sophisticated!). There were cookbooks like *Je Sais Cuisiner*—the French version of *The Joy of Cooking*. And pots and pans of every shape and size—mostly really large. (Peter, so large himself, believed that if really big was good, then really enormous was even better.)

By now, Peter was inviting me for dinner at his apartment, and although we were "just friends," there was an element of seduction in those dinners at the long counter in the kitchen. For one thing, there were dishes I'd never had before. Braised endive, for example. I'd never even heard of endive in those days, much less cooked in something strange called Bovril (brought from trips to visit Elinor, who lived in London) and topped with grated Parmesan. Or discovering that Camembert—which I'd tasted but thought dull—was totally unctuous and delicious. It turned out, of course, that I had never had *good* Camembert—and that was an important life lesson: you can't judge anything until/unless you know it at its best, Peter counseled, one of many wise lessons he preached.

And then there were the menus. In a corner of that kitchen counter was a pile of menus from Peter's favorite restaurants: the Madonna in Venice, Marty's and Chez Georges in Paris, Wheelers in London. These were beloved spots he went to every year. For me, they evoked that magical world I craved. Long before I ever set foot in the Madonna, I dreamt of eating

Tagliatelle al nero di seppia, pasta with squid ink. Or whitebait—miniscule fried fish that melted in your mouth—at Wheelers. Or boudin—blood sausage—at Chez Georges. Remember, this was long before "foodie New York," long before the *New York Times* announced the opening of every trendy new restaurant serving rarified plates on Smith Street or Bedford Avenue. It was a time when French restaurants either served formal old-fashioned classic cuisine à la Escoffier or were tiny bistros whose repertoire centered on coq au vin. It was a time when good bread was just barely beginning to make its appearance. It was a time when the majority of Italian restaurants were red-sauce emporiums. Most Americans had never heard of balsamic vinegar, and cilantro was a rare herb you had to search for. Pesto—what was that? And Whole Foods and Trader Joe's were not a twinkle in anyone's eye. It was a very different time.

Soon dinners in the kitchen had expanded to dinners with Peter's friends—and what friends they were. There were French friends and Spanish friends and Italian friends and British friends, some famous, most not, but it was a glamorous parade of dinner guests to me. With some regularity, Mary Hemingway—Ernest's fourth wife and now widow—swept Peter off to some fancy party or opening, and increasingly, Peter invited me along. Or we'd be asked to dinner at Mary's penthouse apartment where you dined sitting under Miró's painting, *The Farm*. It was right there above your head, familiar and touchable, not hanging on a wall in the National Gallery as it does today.

Where were the children in all of this? At first, I was still "Daddy's friend from Holt," encountered now and then when our paths crossed on weekends, when they were with Peter. Watching their life with Peter was fascinating to me. I had no father growing up (my parents divorced after the war and my father disappeared from the scene). So I was mesmerized by this larger-than-life father who swept his children off to art galleries every Saturday, took them to Europe in the summer one at a time, bought their clothes at Saks in scenes like something out of *Auntie Mame*. These were unselfconsciously sophisticated children who at eight, nine, and eleven could argue about which flavor of sorbet they most adored at Berthillon, the famed *sorbetière* on the Ile St. Louis. They were experienced snorkelers who could stare a barracuda in the face without flinching. They also were warm, funny, smart, affectionate kids.

It's hard to know just when I fell I love with Peter, when realizing that I was totally myself with him turned into realizing that I didn't want to be without him. And along the way, I fell in love with David, Annabel, and Michael, too.

About this time Peter took me on a short trip to the island of St. Barths. This was in 1972, long before St. Barths was a chichi place full of too-rich celebrities. Off-season in the early 1970s, St. Barths was paradise. Flying from St. Martin, we landed on a grass runway where someone had to shoo away the sheep before the plane could touch down. We stayed at a tiny hotel called Eden Roc—which is now very fancy but then was very plain—where the few other guests were French people who came every year. It was the first time I'd ever been with Peter in what was essentially a French world, and as I watched him, something clicked. I understood him in a way I never had before. Drinking wine at a big table on the terrace of Eden Roc, overlooking the moonlit Caribbean, seeing him so at ease, watching the banter (for I really couldn't understand most of it), I saw Peter more comfortable, more of an insider than I had ever seen before. For Peter may have been bilingual in English and French, but he really was far more French than American. He used to say that his passport was American but his soul was French. Suddenly, I got it.

One evening back in New York, after a heavenly dinner, Peter and I were sitting in the living room—me in a sumptuous white leather beanbag chair Peter had shipped back from Paris—when Peter handed me a perfect conch shell. "Tip it," he said. And out of its luminescent pink sliver shimmered the most beautiful gold chain I had ever beheld. As it fell into my hand like golden rain, Peter asked me to marry him. And I said yes. I knew even then that I was accepting a complex man whom many found overbearing, whom some people adored and some avoided. But I also knew that I would never be bored, that I could share my life with someone who always made me laugh, who loved to read as much as I did, and who would show me the world.

A few months later, on May 12, 1973, I walked down the aisle of the chapel at Brick Presbyterian Church in a Mexican wedding dress. Michael was the usher. Annabel was the maid of honor. David was the best man. And my beloved cousin Dottie (she of the first apartment ten years earlier) was matron of honor. A Central Park carriage took us down Park Avenue to the reception at home. There were canapés from a now long-gone shop called Old Denmark and a bathtub filled with ice and bottles of bubbly. It was a wonderful, quirky celebration, filled with love and humor, family and friends, tradition and novelty—just like the life we were about to lead.

Braised Endive

- 6–8 endives
- 6 Tbsp. unsalted butter or olive oil
- Salt and pepper to taste
- 1 Tbsp. Bovril dissolved in 1 cup of boiling water
- Juice of 1 lemon
- Grated Parmesan to cover

Trim the endives by slicing off the base and cutting in half lengthwise.

Heat a large skillet on medium flame. Add the butter and/or olive oil and endive halves. Sprinkle with salt and pepper and sauté the endives until lightly colored (about 2 minutes on each side).

Place endives in a shallow casserole dish. Add Bovril broth* and lemon juice to the butter mixture in the skillet. Bring to a simmer and pour over the endives.

Bake in a 350°F oven until tender (about 25 minutes). Then sprinkle with Parmesan and return to oven until the cheese begins to melt. Place briefly under the broiler to brown the cheese.

*In Peter's original recipe, he used 1 Tbsp. of Bovril, dissolved in 1 cup of boiling water. Bovril is difficult to find, but in its place for added flavor, you could use 1 Tbsp. of freeze-dried miso dissolved in 1 cup of boiling water.

Real Camembert

Buy a real Camembert from someone who knows about cheese, preferably a raw milk Camembert from Normandy, the original Camembert. Ask the cheese merchant to choose one that is ripe, ready to eat. Then serve it at room temperature with pears and a really good baguette—and wine, of course.

POUR LE PLAISIR DES YEUX

As the car bumped and tossed across the rocky, sandy landscape, I thought I was in a giant blender. Ahead of us stretched almost three thousand miles of desert; behind us a sign read "Timbuktu, fifty-four days," with an arrow pointing south. For a moment, I felt as though we had stumbled onto the set of *Lawrence of Arabia*, but sheer terror soon overcame that illusion. I was in a rental car that did not inspire confidence, with Peter—who always inspired confidence, but what did he know about driving across the desert?—and our guide, a small Moroccan boy, who seemed very confident, but I didn't believe a word of it.

It was a Monday morning in 1973 and we were at the end of The Wedding Special, Part II. The Wedding Special was Peter's moniker for a honeymoon, a term he felt was too plebian to be used in polite company. Part I had been a month in the Caribbean. Part II entailed crossing the Atlantic on the *France,* a few days in London (where Peter's mother lived), then three weeks in France, and now another three in Morocco. It was the kind of travel I'd always dreamed of and now it was happening in real life—without my having to be either a missionary or a foreign correspondent!

Our destination was the tiny village of M'Hamid, about thirty-six miles south of Zagora and nine hours south of Marrakech. There was no road, though, just what they call a *piste* in North Africa—a rough, barely visible track across the desert. Riding on a *piste* was a bone-shaking experience. (Later we met some French drivers who were testing Renault cars in the desert. They explained that the *pistes* are made by laying ridged metal down in the sand, which makes it feel like you are driving on a corduroy road. If you drive at a precise speed—something like 60 mph as I remember—then you ride along the tops of the ridges and it's not bumpy.)

I spent the entire trip from Zagora in mortal fear that the boy would lose his way (I could not discern a single landmark anywhere) and/or that we would get stuck in the sand that drifted across the *piste* (a very real possibility). But shaken bones and all, we finally reached M'Hamid where, the *Guide*

Bleu assured us, "the nomad camel-drivers from the desert called the 'Blue People' can be seen in large numbers" at the Monday market.

Once we emerged from our twentieth century automobile, we were in a scene that hadn't changed for who-knows-how-many centuries. In a dusty square surrounded by low mud brick buildings, men in long blue robes bargained over camels and goats in a cacophony of Berber (we assumed, though we couldn't understand a word) and Arabic. We were the only outsiders there, and as I stood against a wall photographing the scene in front of me, I felt as though I had stepped into the *National Geographic* issues of my childhood. Whether it was *Lawrence of Arabia* or *National Geographic*, it was like nothing I had ever experienced before.

Interestingly, no one paid much attention to either Peter or me. The men at the M'Hamid market were conducting serious business. Their lives depended on those camels, and we were irrelevant. It was miles away—literally and figuratively—from a market frequented by tourists, where merchants beseeched you to view their trinkets *pour le plaisir des yeux*, for the pleasure of your eyes.

After a while we could see a lot of camel action past a gate through the walls of the town. Making our way through the crowded square, we emerged into the desert where five or six men were discussing a group of camels. Unlike the bargainers at the market, however, these men took an immediate interest in the tall Americans who had appeared in their midst. "Ah hah," they seemed to say, "there's a little money to be made here," as they eagerly engaged Peter in rapid-fire fractured French. Did he not wish to ride the camels, they asked, since clearly all tourists wanted to ride the camels. Peter laughed—even then, he would have made a heavy weight for a grouchy camel (camels are highly particular about just how much weight they will carry and are known to refuse anything too heavy)—but of course he told them I would be delighted to take a spin on one of their camels. The next thing I knew, one of the men had commanded his camel to kneel, and he was

beckoning me to climb on. Back in my *National Geographic* days, I had read all about camels and I knew that they could be very disagreeable souls. "No thank you," I said. The man smiled broadly and continued to beckon. There was much jovial conversation amongst the camel drivers, and finally I thought, *Okay, I might as well.* So, onto the camel I climbed, as gracefully as I could manage—which was not very graceful at all. The next thing I knew, the camel's owner had very agilely jumped onto the camel saddle behind me. Suddenly several things happened at once: the man called out something to the camel; the camel began to stand up; I tilted forward; and faster than I could say "what in God's name are you doing" in any language, the man had clapped his arms around me, strategically placing one hand on each of my breasts! It was so startling and so inappropriate that all I could do was laugh uproariously. So did Peter and so did the camel contingent (the humans, that is). In short order, the camel took about ten steps, and Peter stopped taking pictures and came to my rescue.

Then, just as I was recovering my equilibrium, a tall Berber man approached us from a tent pitched a short distance from the village walls. Using a combination of gestures and a few French phrases, he invited us to visit him. It was an irresistible invitation. When we reached the tent, he pushed aside the curtain that served as a door and ushered us inside. "*Entrez chez moi*," he said, smiling and inviting us to sit on the ground on dusty velvet cushions. Peter strode right in, as was his wont. I followed, with some trepidation and much fascination. I had never before been in a Berber tent on the edge of the Sahara and I wasn't quite sure how to behave (and being me, of course, I wanted to behave in *just* the right way for the occasion). Our host was a commanding presence, however, and there didn't seem to be any arguing with him.

As we sat, the Berber man spoke curtly to the three heavily veiled women already there. In short order, they and the children who hung onto their robes were outside and we were inside, watching with some concern as our host prepared tea. Although I am far from queasy, the sanitary conditions were suspect at best. *Should we dare eat or drink anything here?* Peter and I both wondered, communicating with worried glances.

The man began by carefully unwrapping three glass cups from a blue velvet bag, speaking rapid-fire Arabic as he proudly showed us each cup. It was clear that they were treasures, though we understood not a word he was saying. His French was limited to a few key phrases, chief among which had been the invitation to come to his tent—a sufficiency, obviously, for there we were, watching in morbid curiosity as he carefully, lovingly wiped each glass with an incredibly dirty cloth that he took from the pocket of his robe.

"Well, at least the water will be boiling," I said hopefully to Peter, sotto voce, as the names of dire and fatal illnesses paraded through my mind. Once having accepted the hospitality of this desert host, there was no way to refuse his tea. Newly married, Peter and I had intentionally embarked on an adventure new to us both. But while Peter had sat in the homes of Otavalos in the Andes and Ibo compounds in Nigeria, nothing had prepared me for this tea party in the Sahara.

Clearly, protocol dictated that making tea was a man's job. As the women chattered rapidly outside the tent, our Berber host boiled the tea water in a copper pot on a tiny brazier. From a tin box, he scooped tea leaves into the copper pot, let it steep for a few minutes, then ceremoniously poured tea into the precious glass cups. As we sipped it, Peter spoke to him in a combination of some French and a lot of sign language, asking where he lived (the answer seemed to be "out there," communicated with a gesture south across the Sahara), what he had come to M'Hamid to do (buy and sell camels), were these his wives and children (yes). When we said we were from New York, the Berber's eyes widened.

Most of the time, I was uncharacteristically silent. I, who can make conversation with a wall, felt oddly out of place. Sitting in the tent in my L. L. Bean khaki pants and jacket (just the right thing for the desert, I had thought), I could hear the women and children outside—the women in their long robes and veils, the children ragged and noisy. Part of me wanted to go out to join them and talk to the women, sorry they had been so gruffly dispatched from the tent. I wish now that I had, but then I was too drawn to the scene inside the tent.

Finally, the tea drunk, the limits of conversation reached, we arose. Peter shook hands with our host as he thanked him in French. I sensed somehow that shaking hands with a woman was not part of Berber etiquette, so I smiled, nodded my head, and expressed effusive thanks. Then we stepped out into the fierce sunlight. The market was over, so we headed back to the car. In those days, outsiders rarely ventured as far as M'Hamid—we had been the only ones that day—so we were a curiosity wherever we walked in the village. At the car, our faithful young cicerone was holding forth to a crowd of children, taking great pride in his "official" position as guide to the visiting Americans. As we bounced our way back to Zagora along the *piste,* I knew I had never in my life been farther away from anything I'd ever known before.

We'd started this adventure ten days earlier in Marrakech. Today the cities of Morocco are crowded with package tours, but then there were few tourists and even fewer who ventured off the beaten path (literally, in the case of our trip to M'Hamid). Since we intended to spend all of our time in Marrakech in the souks—the rabbit warren of streets that made up the markets—even super-independent Peter recognized that we needed a guide. So our first morning at the

Hotel Mamounia—then still more like the place Winston Churchill loved to stay than the glitzy jet-set hotel it is now—Peter approached the concierge. He explained that we would be using a guide for a full week, that at the end of the week we would undoubtedly buy some treasures, but that under no circumstances did we want to be taken in and out of shops for the first five or six days. Reassured emphatically that this would not happen, we set out with the recommended guide. It didn't work. The official guides of Marrakech must have magnets in their shoes, for they were completely incapable of avoiding the shops. "Just see these rugs," our man said. "*Pour le plaisir des yeux.*" "We don't want to buy anything now, for the pleasure of our eyes or not," Peter boomed, but to no avail. In the afternoon of Day One, we fired our guide.

We spent the rest of that day in the extraordinary Place Jemaa el Fna. The *place* looked like a North African version of a medieval fair. In the morning it was filled with tradesmen (no women) selling fruits and vegetables. Barbers were cutting hair and giving shaves. One man came every day with his small bathroom scale. He earned his living by allowing people to weigh themselves for one *dirhan* (then worth about a quarter). There were scribes, too. Men who could not read or write sat earnestly in front of them, dictating letters to be sent or having them read documents that they then signed. By the afternoon, the square turned into a festival of performers. Black acrobats from south of the Sahara turned handstands. Indian men played flutes to make their cobras dance. Moroccan musicians played instruments that sounded exotic to our ears. And scattered around the square were storytellers who told one part of their story all day long, storyteller and listeners all sitting on the ground in a circle. The next day, the storyteller moved on to the next chapter, and on and on every day until it was time to begin a new story.

In the fall of 1973, the few tourists who ventured near the Place Jemaa el Fna scurried up to the rooftop of the Café de la Glaciére, at the edge of the square, where they could look at this amazing scene "in safety." We went to the café too, but to recover from the Place Jemaa el Fna, not to escape it. Sitting in the café by the end of that first day we were exhilarated, exhausted, and puzzled. How were we going to navigate the souks without a guide?

As we sat drinking the ubiquitous mint tea, we heard "psst" down by Peter's elbow. "Psst" It was coming from a small, scruffy teenage boy squatting beside us. "I am Mustafa," he introduced himself in not-very-good French. He was a student, he said. Every male of a certain age claimed he was a student, we soon learned. "Do you need a guide?" he asked, and named a modest daily rate. Peter and I looked at one another, looked at the sweet and earnest face of the scruffy boy, and said "*Oui, bien sur,*" in one voice. It was agreed that we would meet Mustafa at the café the next morning, that he would take us to the souks all day, and that shopping was not in the picture until later.

The next day was heaven. Mustafa knew everywhere to go. Like the Place Jemaa el Fna, the souks were like something out of the Middle Ages. You walked along a street crowded with the people of Marrakech, shops and workshops on cither side, straw mats covering the sky overhead. One street was nothing but shops making and selling jewelry. On another, every open door revealed boys pounding metal to make cooking pots. On another, there were weavers. And on and on.

By late afternoon, Peter and I were delightedly walking down yet another street, gaily colored yarns drying above our heads, when suddenly, out of nowhere, two Marrakech policemen swept down upon us, grabbed Mustafa by the arm, and dragged him away, shouting in Arabic. We were stunned. What in heaven's name had just happened?

After a restorative cup of mint tea at the café, we trudged to the edge of the square where our car was parked. As we sat in the car thinking "now what?" we heard a familiar "psst." Sure enough, crouching down next to the car was Mustafa, looking the worse for wear (and rough handling), but plucky as ever. He explained the problem: he was not an official guide of course, and the association of guides and the police were ever on the lookout for unofficial guides like Mustafa. Being an unofficial guide was strictly against the law, he said. Ever resourceful, however, Mustafa had a plan. And sure enough, for the remainder of our week in Marrakech, it worked. Having mutually decided on an agenda for each day, Mustafa would walk ahead of us, never looking back at us but directing a stream of information and directions over his shoulder. We followed, never letting him out of our sight and highly amused by the whole escapade. It worked brilliantly.

When it was almost time for us to leave for the south, Mustafa told us that his mother was very grateful that we were helping her son. She would like for us to come to dinner. We accepted instantly, realizing what an honor it was for Mustafa's mother to feel comfortable in inviting American strangers into her home. On the appointed day, Mustafa picked us up at the café and led us—always walking ahead—back into a neighborhood we had never seen. Tiny mud brick houses crowded around small courtyards. Off one little courtyard, sitting on the ground in front of her two-room house, was Mustafa's mother. In front of her was a small brazier covered with what looked like a dented pie tin. Over and over she put her hand into a bowl of batter and tapped it lightly across the hot tin. The minute she finished covering the tin, she began peeling off a sheet of pastry like a paper-thin crepe. She was making the pastry for a dish called *bstila*, layers of something like phyllo dough, stuffed with chicken—sometimes pigeon—and spices. According to Mustafa, she had once worked in the kitchen of the king in Rabat and was famous for her *bstila*. While Peter sat and tried to talk with Mustafa's mother, whose French was minimal, Mustafa and I went to a nearby market where he bought a live chicken to be killed and dressed at home and baked in the *bstila*.

For the rest of the day, we played our "follow Mustafa" game and then that night we dined on *bstila* in the home of Mustafa. The *bstila* was divine, one of the most delicious things I have ever consumed. The delicate, crispy layers crackled as you bit into a filling of chicken, cinnamon, ginger, and saffron. When I think back on the entire scene, I realize that Mustafa's mother must have baked this in a communal oven in their neighborhood, for there was no sign of an oven in their miniscule house.

As we ate, Mustafa's mother shyly stood to the side, refusing to eat with us, only serving. His older brother and sister were a different matter. Both were far more educated than Mustafa (who probably hadn't been a student for many years). Listening to them talk bitterly about the French, the king, and the rights they felt deprived of, you could imagine even then a future Arab Spring. We had brought presents—I no longer remember what—but the greatest present was Mustafa's trust in us, to bring us to his home.

The night before we left Marrakech, we had one other memorable meal, very different from the dinner at Mustafa's. A close Parisian friend, who grew up in Casablanca, had given us the name of a Marrakech jeweler. We'd gone to his quiet, elegant shop several times, to look at and learn about the traditional and antique Moroccan jewelry he collected and sold: heavy silver bracelets covered with engraving, gold-washed bracelets inlaid with semiprecious stones, silver pendants colored with colored enamels, pins for holding robes. After several visits to the shop, we picked out some beautiful pieces to buy—a thick gold-wash bracelet and a delicately filigreed pendant.

The jeweler was a scholar of his trade, a soft-spoken but confident purveyor of treasures and knowledge who was completely different from the men who so aggressively hawked their wares on the streets. So, when he invited us for dinner, we were fascinated to see his home and meet his family. He lived on a tree-lined street in a part of town that spanned the old town and the modern, colonial city. But once inside his house, there was no question: you were in a middle-class, traditional Moroccan home. At the center was a courtyard with a delicate marble fountain, playing the music of the Arab world—the gentle sound of falling water.

It happened to be the night of Eid al-Fitr, the end of Ramadan, a night for celebration and feasting. We sat on soft cushions on the floor and ate at a low table with the family—the jeweler, his wife, and his children. The children were struck dumb by these large French-speaking Americans, but the jeweler and his shy but gracious wife made us feel completely at home as they explained each dish of the delicious meal. Now forty years later, it all blurs into one large tajine in my memory. A tajine, named for the dish in which it is served, is one of the most basic Moroccan dishes—stew in a wide variety of guises—lamb, chicken, or beef with vegetables and spices.

The next morning, we left Marrakech, first going south to Zagora and M'Hamid, scene of that memorable Berber tea party, then west across the Atlas Mountains. We stopped at a medieval-century castle in the middle of nowhere. We visited a village at the edge of the Sahara on a festival day when the streets were crowded with sheep and goats and more women than we had ever seen in one place in all of Morocco. We drove south to a vast swath of sand dunes that were breathtaking in their undulating rusty-red glory. There in an almost stereotypical moment, a small boy appeared at the top of a dune, waving a stick and shouting frantically. "I've lost my camels," he cried as he approached (this according to the village boy who had taken us out to the dunes). We had not seen his camels, we regretfully informed him. He disappeared over the dune, still waving his stick.

In that transit between Marrakech and Fez, we also declined someone's hospitality for the one and only time. The gentle young man who took us to the dunes invited us to stop at his home on the way back to our hotel. When we arrived, his mother came in to offer us tea. In her arms was a thin and crying baby, whose eyes were covered in mucus, the sign of a dread eye disease that was rampant in parts of Morocco. As politely but emphatically as we could, we told her son (she spoke no French) that we could not possibly accept her offer, making up some excuse that we only prayed he would believe.

When we reached our second Moroccan city, Fez, we settled in for a magical week. It could not have been more different than Marrakech. Where Marrakech was sandy and hot and golden brown, Fez was stony and cool and gray. Marrakech felt like a desert, Fez like the mountains.

Once again, we spent all of our time in "the old city," wandering the souks and returning at night to our elegant but traditional hotel. In Fez, it was the Palais Jamaï, an elegant nineteenth-century palace set up on one of the hills of the old city, overlooking the medina and the hills beyond. It was Peter's kind of place, too—swarming with staff, most of whom gave a small bow whenever they encountered him (I just rolled my eyes).

And at long last, we had the perfect guide. Ralli Rais—I can still see him in his miraculously immaculate white *djalaba* with a red fez atop his head. Ralli instantly understood our request not to shop until the end, bowed slightly, and took us in hand as only a truly knowledgeable guide can do. Every morning he appeared at the hotel with an agenda of treasures to see: the vast olive market; a school classroom where we brought complete, awed silence to a room full of nine-year-olds; the alleys of dyers and weavers where a wonder of colored yarns hung drying overhead; the tanneries, where Ralli gave me a bouquet of fresh mint to hold in front of my nose to counter the incredibly noxious fumes; the mosques into which we could only peek.

Every night, Peter and I read aloud to one another from a slim volume called *Fez in the Age of the Marinides*, which described Fez in the fourteenth century. The next morning, Ralli Rais showed us his city—almost exactly the same place we had read about the night before, a medieval city before our eyes. In the 1300s, "near the river were found the workshops of weavers, shoemakers, makers of brass ware, blacksmiths, and so forth." Sure enough, they were still there. We'd read about the craftsmen who made copper vessels and the rope makers who braided hemp ropes. Then we saw the same things the next day. As the *Guide Bleu* said, it was a city that "preserved intact . . . the physiognomy of Islam's medieval towns."

Each night around midnight, a haunting sound filled our hotel room. Five times a day, we could hear the muezzins calling the faithful to prayer, each with a different voice—the calls were human then, not recorded as they usually are today. We wondered what this special and beautiful song was. Ralli, fount of all knowledge, explained that it was a man who came to one mosque every night, to sing a song to comfort those who could not sleep. He was a butcher by day, a soother of souls by night.

Ralli took us to his home for lunch every day, dismissing as inappropriate for us either local restaurants or the tourist spots (few in those days). Every day his wife served us what she insisted was their "regular lunch." And it was always delicious: couscous in every permutation, lamb tagines that were different every day, a salad of oranges and carrots, and the breads—warm and puffy and divine.

Ralli and his wife showed us how to eat with the index finger and thumb of your right hand. "*Ah, d'accord*," I said as I spilled copious amounts of couscous down my front. She also offered to take me to the local baths, the hammam, an offer I was too shy to accept—to my eternal regret.

At the end of the week, we drove from Fez to Casablanca, where we would leave for home. Awaiting us in Casablanca, however, was one more memorable meal. The same elegant Parisian who had sent us to the Marrakech jeweler had given us an introduction to her brother, who was the owner of one of the major newspapers in Casablanca. When Peter called him, he invited us to a dinner party the following night.

All I can say is that "*le tout Maroc*" was at that party. There was the most recent ambassador to the United States, a newly appointed director of the World Bank, plus assorted diplomats, newspaper editors, and socialites. It was enough to make me womperjawed, as Peter's mother would have said. We were the only non-Moroccans there and decidedly the least chic. One woman was more elegantly dressed—in Parisian haute couture—than the next. Air kissing abounded. Everyone slid smoothly from Arabic to French to English to Spanish. Everyone smiled tolerantly as I spoke my fractured French.

The meal was equally grand, though the hostess insisted that this was a simple, casual dinner for friends. When we were called to dinner, we found a room with a row of liveried servants each standing behind a towering tajine, larger than any I had ever seen. As you approached, said servant lifted the top of the tajine to show you its contents and to serve you if you wished.

At the end of that evening I thought back on the incredible span of meals that we had had in our three Moroccan weeks—from tea in a Berber tent to liveried servants in Casablanca. But there was no question in either Peter's mind or mine. The most wonderful moment, the one we would treasure forever, was eating *bstila* in the tiny house of Mustafa.

La Bstila de Francoise Firmin

The year before we were married, our Parisian friend Francoise spent a year in New York, during which she undertook to teach me how to cook (and made futile attempts to improve my French accent). Francoise had grown up in Casablanca and, in her New York kitchen, she produced a real bstila, *my very first. This makes 8 servings.*

Water, just to cover the chicken
1 cup plus 2 Tbsp. salted butter
Salt to taste
1 small onion, chopped
2 tsp. ground ginger powder
1 tsp. *ras el hanout* spice*
Pinch of saffron
2½ tsp. cinnamon, *divided*
Fresh coriander and parsley, a handful of each, with stems
8 chicken wings plus 4 chicken thighs
10 eggs, plus 2 eggs for assembling the *bstila*
1 cup almonds, blanched, skinned, and chopped
18 sheets of phyllo pastry
⅔–¾ cup sugar

Begin by preparing the stuffing.

In a Dutch oven, place water, butter (reserving 2 Tbsp. for roasting the almonds), several pinches of salt, chopped onion, ginger, *ras el hanout*, saffron, a little less than half of the cinnamon, and coriander and parsley. Melt the butter and saute the mixture briefly. Add the chicken and just enough water to cover. Bring to a boil, then simmer gently until the meat falls off the bone. Remove the chicken from the liquid, saving the broth. When the meat has cooled to the touch, remove from the bone.

Divide the chicken broth in half. Reheat one half but do not let it boil. Remove from heat and beat in 10 eggs, one at a time. The mixture will thicken as the eggs cook in the hot liquid.

Reduce the other half of the chicken broth to a glaze.

Lightly roast the almonds in 2 Tbsp. of butter.

Now you are ready to construct the *bstila.*

You should have close at hand:

- Phyllo, wrapped in a damp dishtowel, as it dries out very quickly
- 2 eggs well beaten to serve as "glue" for the phyllo
- The remaining cinnamon
- Chopped almonds
- Chicken meat (detached from the bones)
- Egg/broth mixture
- Chicken broth glaze
- Sugar

Choose a platter large enough to serve as a base for the round *bstila* you will create. Cover a rimless baking sheet with parchment or foil to replicate the size of your platter; you will bake the *bstila* on this. Place 6 phyllo sheets on the baking sheet, brushing each sheet with the beaten egg wash. Sprinkle sugar over this base of phyllo.

Mix the almonds with the remaining cinnamon and place on the phyllo. Pile up half of the egg/broth mixture and cover with some of the glaze. Cover this with 6 more phyllo sheets, again brushing each sheet with the beaten egg wash. Spread the chicken meat mixture, the remaining egg/broth mixture, and the remaining glaze over the phyllo.

Cover with 6 more phyllo sheets, brushing each sheet with egg wash. Tuck phyllo in and around to create a nice round shape. Brush the whole *bstila* with the egg wash.

Cook for about 30 minutes at 375°F until the pastry is golden brown. Slide the *bstila* onto the platter.

Serve with couscous cooked in broth with golden raisins and/or apricots.

*If you cannot find *ras el hanout* locally, you can order it online. It is a mixture of spices and other ingredients. Be sure to get one that includes rose petals; this is key to the flavor!

Moroccan Chicken

In a bookstore in Fez, we found a copy of Fez: Traditional Moroccan Cooking, *translated from the French, and when we got home—our heads filled with images and memories and tastes of Morocco—we tried and adapted a few recipes. This was one of them—though, I must confess, we ordered our chicken from the butcher, contrary to the original recipe's instructions to "slaughter, pluck, draw, and wash it"!*

1 cup butter, plus more for couscous and to brown chicken
1 cup steamed couscous
⅓ cup almonds, coarsely chopped
½ cup raisins, chopped
1 scant tsp. *ras el hanout*
1 large chicken
Pinch of powdered ginger
1 onion, chopped
1 tsp. salt
Pinch of saffron pounded with salt

Add 2 Tbsp. of butter to the steamed couscous. Mix in the almonds, raisins, and *ras el hanout* to make a stuffing.

Loosely stuff the chicken and sew the opening closed.

In a Dutch oven, place a pinch of powdered ginger, chopped onion, 1 tsp. salt, and the saffron/salt mixture.

Place the chicken in a cooking pan, half cover with water, and place on high heat. When the water boils, add 6 Tbsp. butter.

Simmer uncovered until meat falls easily off the bone and most, but not all, of the water has evaporated. Add butter to the remaining water as needed to brown the chicken on all sides.

The way to eat this dish, the Fez cookbook advises, is first to rub the chicken with a piece of bread, then dip the bread in the sauce and "enjoy this savoury morsel." Then take the chicken meat "delicately with the tips of your finger, break the breast bone and attack the stuffing, golden and sweet with a flavor which will surprise and astonish the most jaded palate."

VAUT LE VOYAGE

Early one golden October morning in 1973, I found myself racing through France's Loire Valley in the back of an open Jeep, flanked by two sleek Brittany spaniels, their ears flying. At the wheel—well, his hands were on the wheel when they were not in Gallic action enthusiastically making some point—was Jean Troisgros, the hottest three-star chef in France at the time. As Jean told Peter about each farmer at the tiny outdoor market where we were headed, I let the sea of French roll right over my head while I happily pondered how in the world I, Susan Grace Washburn Buckley, had ended up in that Jeep.

The adventure had begun a few weeks earlier. Landing in Paris on The Wedding Special, Part II, I was in France with Peter for the first time, in the place he considered home. Our first stop going into town was of course, to have a meal. We went to a tiny bistro Peter had known forever, where he insisted on ordering what he called the truly classic French meal, *steak frites*. No rich sauces, no foie gras, no cream, just a simple *steak frites*—the best steak and "French fries" I had ever had.

"Now we're in civilization," Peter proclaimed, raising a glass of some (delicious) *vin ordinaire*. "What do you mean?" I contested. "Isn't London civilized too?" I said, thinking of our recent visit. "You'll see," he said confidently, and he was right.

For the next four or five days we barreled around Paris in our rented car, Peter showing me the places he and his mother had lived in Paris during their European peregrinations between 1926 and 1938; where he'd seen the Punch and Judy show in the Tuileries as a little boy; where he'd gone to school in the thirties; where he'd driven his army jeep straight up the stairs in front of the Sacré-Cœur at the liberation of Paris. He took me to his favorite haunts, small restaurants like Allard with its renowned coq au vin. We went to "Heaven," Peter's name for Berthillon, home of the world's best sorbet. And one night we went out to the tiny new restaurant outside of Paris where Michel Guérard was experimenting with what was becoming known as *la nouvelle cuisine*. It was the hot new spot everyone wanted to go to, tiny and crowded, but filled with *le tout Paris.* In a slightly surreal appearance, Danny Kaye arrived, completely manic and wearing bright blue suede shoes. Everyone was so close together that Peter and Danny Kaye were soon trading jokes to the bemusement of the more formal French diners who were trying to figure out this strange minimalist but fantastic food, this tiny crowded restaurant, and these two crazy Americans (Peter and Danny Kaye).

And then there were Peter's Paris friends, one more fascinating and appealing to me than the next. We stayed with surgeon Paul Tessier, who lived in an immense apartment off the Arc de Triomphe when he wasn't flying around the world "surging." We played with Francis and Francoise, also surgeons, whom we'd grown to love when they spent a year in New York. Francoise and Peter, equally naughty, incited outrageous behavior in one another to an alarming degree, while Francis and I rolled our eyes but secretly loved every minute of it. Jean-Pierre and another Francoise were Peter's friends from college days, and it was in their home that I decided to speak French no matter how badly it came out. They were so lovely, so witty and sophisticated, but also so welcoming that, as I sat there looking like a simp, only saying *oui, non, merci,* I thought, *If I am afraid to speak French with people as generous as these, I'll never have fun in France.* So I began to talk (as is my wont), making all manner of mistakes, but warmly encouraged by Jean-Pierre and Francoise. As Peter would later say, "Susan speaks a lot of French words." My grammar was terrible, but my vocabulary grew like Topsy. I was so motivated that I was like a sponge. "Use the glazed eye approach," Peter advised. When I got in over my head and started making incomprehensible statements, people's eyes would glaze over and it was time to call in the experts.

After Paris we went first to Mont Saint-Michel, which provided sustenance for the soul. But then we began an outrageously indulgent parade from one three-star restaurant to another. The Michelin tire company has been awarding one, two, or three stars to outstanding restaurants since 1926, with three stars for a restaurant whose cuisine is so good that it's worth a special trip, *ca vaut le voyage*. In 1973 there were sixteen three-star restaurants in all of France—more than any year before. (In 2016 there were hundreds of three-star restaurants around the world, from Spain to South Korea, with more in Japan [thirty-two] than in France [twenty-six].) In 1973, though each of the sixteen three-star restaurants was a temple of gastronomy, none were as chichi or as breathtakingly expensive as they are today, when as one friend observed, you have to take a Brink's truck of money to afford a dinner for two. Still, our having five three-star meals within the space of about ten days was beyond excessive. As I was to discover, however, the experience was about much more than just food. This was about Food—and the service that went with it. This was my introduction to a culture in which fine dining was an art form. And like the trip to St. Barths, it was a window into Peter's French soul.

Just planning this gastronomic extravaganza had opened my eyes to a new world of eating. The spring before the trip Peter had sat at his desk in New York, surrounded by Michelin maps, the red Michelin guide, and the latest roster of Michelin-starred restaurants. In those days, Michelin stars mattered more than they probably do today, when the world posts its every opinion online. But then, the 1972 list merited a special to the *New York Times* with a headline questioning, "Will the

Guide Michelin Reach for a Fourth Star?" (They didn't.) The article cited "everyone's favorites: the Troisgros brothers at Roanne, Paul Bocuse at Lyons, and the Haeberlins at Illhaeusern in Alsace." Peter proposed—with my enthusiastic agreement—that we should head for Roanne and Lyons as part of a Wedding Special visit to Burgundy.

On our way south we stopped first in Tours to visit the newly three-starred restaurant of Charles Barrier. A shy man, Barrier wasn't a chef much talked about, but the *Times* article had noted that he was baking his own bread, much to everyone's amazement. (In the bread-besotted world we live in today, it's hard to believe that this was worthy of describing in the *Times*. But then, that was an era when French bakers reigned supreme. . . . Bakers baked and chefs "cheffed.")

Barrier was the least exciting of the three-star restaurants we went to on that trip, but it was my very first experience in true haute cuisine and I was very excited. I felt a little like a movie star or someone equally glamorous as the maître d'hôtel seated us with dignity. This was just the beginning of my understanding of what it meant to serve in a traditional restaurant in France, where being a waiter is a respected profession, not a job between acting gigs, and service is ingrained in everyone. Not subservience but service that pays homage to the seriousness of the undertaking—to the creation of a meal worthy of a star—or two or three.

I loved everything about it. It wasn't serious in a pretentious way, though it could have seemed silly to many people, but if you accepted the value of spending time and money on eating exquisite food, then it was all of a piece, from the person who seated you to the time you took to discuss dishes and wines, from the elegance of the menu itself, to the low hum of happy diners in the beautifully decorated dining room.

I remember with amusement that I felt a certain awe, as if I were in a cathedral, speaking quietly and holding myself with some formality. This was not going to be just a good meal; it was going to be a kind of sacred communion. But of course, it was just a really, really good meal, with flavors I had never encountered before. The first night I had some extraordinary terrine made with three local fishes, a fish from the Loire, chicken with tarragon sauce, and the famous breads, which Barrier paired with each course as if they were fine wines. And later, the most fabulous Calvados I had ever tasted. The second dinner was even better: a duck liver terrine, a local fish, beef with shallots (only mediocre), and exquisite Crepes Gil Blas, of which I remember only the name and that they were lighter and more delicious than any crepes had a right to be. (If I hadn't written all of this down, I wouldn't believe that we had four courses each night.) Incredibly, we finished with a Vouvray sorbet and tiny glasses of framboise. I am uncertain as to how we found our way back to the hotel, but we made it back somehow.

We stayed in Tours for a few days after that, spending our days driving through the gorgeous countryside from one exquisite château to another, all out of a storybook. Chenonceau, like a bridge across the Loire. Blois, which we saw on a foggy day when the towers of the château emerged from the fog like a castle in a mirage and where you imagined you could hear the sounds of a boar hunt in the distance. This may have been because Peter was remembering the time he went on a boar hunt, on horseback, nearby. It was a country weekend with the family of his friend from college days, Elizabeth Roth le Gentil, an impossibly glam Salvadorian coffee heiress who had married a Frenchman. All of the glamour was melding together in my mind by this time: imagining Peter on horseback hunting wild boar, dreaming of life in one of the châteaux, savoring my first three-star meal. As the new bride, I soaked it all up while I pinched myself to wonder whether I had wandered into a novel or not.

Adding to the fairytale were encounters like the morning we saw a farmer and his wife standing in a meadow in front of a half-timbered barn. It looked as though it was built in the Renaissance and we discovered that it had been. They had just come in from the woods where they were searching for cèpes, the giant mushrooms they collected and sold to the purveyor who came down from Paris once a week to buy whatever they had found, to sell to one great Parisian chef or another.

On another ride along the river we stopped in front of a charming house while Peter remembered the days when he visited his friend, the sculptor Jo Davidson, who'd lived there. When we came to a tiny inn nearby, Peter spun out a tale of dancing with Alexander Calder, who was married to Davidson's daughter. I could just see them like two giant bears (both men were of an ursine size and shape), singing joyously after consuming way too much wine. It is a picture I have always treasured.

The most memorable experience on that three-star trip, however, began when we reached Roanne and Les Frères Troisgros. Roanne then was a dusty town on the route south from Paris to the Mediterranean with the ubiquitous and unprepossessing small hotels clustered around the railroad station. One of these had been owned by the Troisgros family for several generations. The hotel was small and old-fashioned and so was the dining room. I remember a lot of brown wood and khaki walls and nineteenth-century oil paintings. But the décor was the only thing old-fashioned in 1973, for by then two young Troisgros brothers—Jean and Pierre—were becoming world-famous, along with their Lyonnaise pal, Paul Bocuse. The first of the celebrity chefs, all three were young, exuberant, witty, and immensely talented.

Now we were in serious three-star mode. Because we were staying at the Troisgros hotel, Peter asked to see a menu in the afternoon after we arrived. Sitting with cups of tea in the hotel's tiny bar area, we poured over the two-page *carte*. Unlike menus at other "fancy" restaurants I'd ever been to, this had only one page listing dishes, with a facing page showing what the French call a "menu," which is a proposed set of courses at a fixed price. (We never ordered the set menu; that would have been much too unadventurous for either one of us.)

I still have that 1973 menu, covered with notes and questions in Peter's bold writing: lines crossing out items we didn't want, questions next to some dishes ("what herbs?" "with cheese?"). We were like two generals with their battle plans: well, if you have x tonight, I could have y, and then I could have z tomorrow, and on and on.

After an obligatory nap—after all, preparation was required for the culinary marathon to come—we dressed for dinner, then went to the lounge where we had something light like a kir and discussed the menu with the maître d'hôtel and the sommelier, who observed that Peter knew what he was doing when he ordered the wine.

On the back of the Troisgros menu Peter wrote down what we had for that first night's dinner. For Peter, it was *Le Choix de Terrines Panachées, L'Escalope de Truite Saumonée à l'Oseille Troisgros*, and *Faison*: a selection of terrines or pâtés clearly with panache; then salmon trout, one of their specialties, cooked with some kind of sorrel sauce; and the *Gibiers de Saison*, which must have been pheasant.

I had *Feuilleté de Ris de Veau, Bar Poché Sauce Antiboise,* and *Le Château Fleurie à la Moelle.* I can still see the thin "leaves" of sweetbreads nestled in the lightest imaginable puff pastry shells with some exquisite cream sauce. The *bar* (sea bass) had a tomato and herb sauce that was full of surprises like cilantro—who ever imagined sea bass with tomato sauce in the first place but never with cilantro, which was a flavor I associated with Mexican and Chinese food; and the most fabulous, a chateaubriand cooked in Beaujolais with marrow. The perfectly pink meat was cut in thick juicy slices, with pieces of poached beef marrow laid across the top of the meat, all surrounded by a pond (I was going to say "sea" but that would not be delicate enough for what this looked like) of a red wine sauce that had all of the delicacy of Fleurie, my favorite-named of the ten Beaujolais Cru vintages.

Finally, for dessert—was there really room after all of this??—we chose from *Le Grand Dessert*, which was a dessert cart with an amazing array of goodies as only the French can dream up. I only remember the cart and my eyes glazing over. And, of course, all this was accompanied by wines carefully chosen by Peter and the sommelier. I am sure it was a two-bottle dinner, as we had to drive nowhere. Each of these dishes was totally, incredibly, amazingly divine. Decades later I still remember that each one tasted better than anything I'd ever put in my food-loving mouth before.

And the service: the overused adjective would be "impeccable," but that doesn't begin to describe it. The service at Barrier was impeccable, "correct" as the French would say. But at Troisgros there was something different—a warmth that welcomed you to the perfectly set table and the skilled serving of each dish with its accompanying cutlery. Perhaps it came about because the Troisgros family had been at this game for two generations, beginning when Troisgros *mère* was in charge of the kitchen. Perhaps it was because this was a small provincial town, not a grand city filled with tourists. For whatever reason, it never felt stiff or pretentious. You had a sense that the waiters were as proud of the food they were serving as we were excited to eat it. The French call the group who work together in a restaurant *l'équipe*, the team. And that is what those waiters felt like.

Finally, happily stuffed, we left the dining room to go to our room. Because it was an old establishment, not yet made fancy, this required walking through an anteroom just off the kitchen. And there, dressed in his traditional black-and-white checked trousers and white jacket, was Jean Troisgros himself, playing cards with a white-haired woman whom we quickly ascertained was his mother. In his inimitable fashion Peter said (in French, of course) something like "Madame Troisgros, your son has just given me the most exquisitely delicious meal I have ever consumed, in a long life of great meals." In my memory, I think he gave Jean and his mother a little bow, but that hardly seems possible. Troisgros *mère et fils* were instantly fascinated by this large man with the booming voice who spoke perfect colloquial French. And the next thing I knew, we were sitting at the table with the mother and son, drinking brandy and talking about food. It was that conversation that landed me in the Jeep on the way to the market the next morning.

As we left the table, a lovely red-haired American student came down the stairs. She'd recently arrived from St. Louis, to spend a year with the Troisgros family. It was Judy Rodgers, she of Zuni Café fame many years later. I remember being deeply envious of the year she was about to have.

The next morning, we set out early, before the women of Roanne came to do their marketing. At each stand, the farmers, the butchers, and the cheesemakers were still laying out their goods: Carrots and leeks and tomatoes in perfect rows, arrayed like a still life. Cheeses sitting on straw or grape leaves each with a tiny identifying sign attached on a toothpick. The fishmonger and the butcher, knives at the ready to produce just the fillet or cut demanded.

Peter and I trailed behind Jean as he greeted one purveyor after another. "*Ah Jean, ça va?*" they called out. He knew them all, and some had known him since he was a boy, going to this same market with his mother, the first Troisgros chef (though never a three-star celebrity like her sons).

Peter had spent his life going to French markets and I'd seen a few by this time, but never like this: going to a local market with one of the world's most accomplished chefs, watching what he chose, how he headed for particular vendors whom he'd known all his life and who had set aside their very best for him.

Three-star chefs like Troisgros do not do casual marketing. Their menus are planned long in advance, centered on dishes they have created and whose ingredients they can count on having. The best greengrocers and butchers and fishmongers in the region deliver the best of the best to the restaurant every day. But this day at the market Troisgros sought out special treasures like a particular goat cheese he wanted to serve that night. Heading for one woman's small stand, he greeted her warmly. After they shook hands and we were introduced, they discussed his mother's health and her mother's health and what had happened to the prize goat who was off her feed last week. After the obligatory "catching up," the woman handed Jean a wooden box with three or four small cheeses. Troisgros smiled broadly, shook her hand again, and we were off to the next stop as he explained the rare virtues of this cheese, which the cheesemaker didn't often make (for some arcane reason that escaped my French comprehension completely). At dinner that night, when the waiter rolled around the cheese cart with its array of twenty to thirty different cheeses, these would be pointed out as a special local delicacy. And Peter and I would smile knowingly to one another, remembering the market woman and the warm morning banter.

There were a few more stops, one to buy some enormous mushrooms, cèpes, like those we saw in the Loire Valley that an old woman collected in the woods and sent to the market with a neighboring farmer, especially for Jean.

One last visit, to Jean's wine merchant where the distiller of eau-de-vie was in residence for his seasonal visit. A few times a year, when the fruit was just ripe, the distiller came to town, with his alembic, a magical-looking copper contraption in which generations of his family had distilled grapes for marc, pears for *poire*, raspberries for framboise, plums for prunelle, and all of the other delicious distillations of fruit that become *alcool blanc* or eau-de-vie: "water of life." Mashed fruit is heated in the bottom of the alembic, and the vapors twist and turn through a spider web of tiny pipes until they turn back into liquid—a clear liquid with an alcohol count of 40 percent and flavors like nothing else. As Jean and the distiller talked about the relative merits of the pears from Monsieur X and those from Madame Y, and Peter joined in with stories about the time just after the war when he went on a day's journey in Alsace, tasting *poire* and framboise at every farmhouse, until he and his car staggered home miraculously intact.

Too soon, we got back in the Jeep, I tucked myself in between the spaniels (who had waited for us patiently), and we were off to the restaurant. It was about 9:00 a.m. by this time, and Jean had a three-star lunch to oversee.

Of all the many three-star restaurants I was lucky enough to go to over the years, those first meals at Troisgros were my favorite by far. We would go back to Les Frères Troisgros twice more over the years—once in 1976 and one last time in the 1980s after Jean had died of a heart attack and when Pierre reigned alone over a super-fancy kitchen and a super-fancy dining room filled with super-fancy people. He greeted us warmly, remembering our first visit and his irrepressible brother. When Peter thanked him for what he did for his happy patrons, Pierre smiled a little sadly as he talked of his brother and then said, "Ah, Monsieur Buckley, *c'est une acte humanitaire*"—a humanitarian act—to cook like this. We nodded in fond but solemn agreement.

That first year, though, nothing was super-fancy. It was just super-incredible food. It was the quintessence of what three Michelin stars really mean—or meant then at least: food as an art, flavors so delicate but so unctuous and so rich (the flavors, not the food), hours at the table, wines perfectly paired with each course, and service that was perfection, with waiters so smoothly professional that they made you feel as though your experience was the most important thing in the world. And unlike today when the cost of this is insane and it all seems like a hedonistic indulgence, those meals forty years ago felt like special, treasured occasions.

Lyons was next. On that first visit I fell in love with the city with its two rivers—the standing joke, though, is that three rivers flow through Lyons: the Rhône, the Saône, and the Beaujolais—amazing markets, and delicious food at every turn. But our holy grail for that trip was two dinners at the restaurant of Paul Bocuse. Before we'd left Roanne, Jean

Troisgros had opined that his friend Paul Bocuse had to be very careful. "We have to please our neighbors in Roanne, who come to us frequently," Jean said. "And they *know* what our cuisine is supposed to taste like. But Paul is in Lyons, and he doesn't have to please his neighbors. His clientele is mostly tourists." He shrugged as if to say, "and you know what they know (or don't know) . . ."

Nevertheless, if one chef epitomizes the 1970s era of celebrity chefs, it is Paul Bocuse. His roots in Lyons are deep. He is the seventh generation of his family to cook on the banks of the Saône River in Collonges-au-Mont-d'Or, a tiny village outside of Lyons.

Filled with anticipation, we drove out from Lyons on an early October evening. The setting was bucolic—the river, the soft golden light at the end of the day. The glowing dining room looked like the French country inn that it had been, with an enormous fireplace at one end in which roasting meats and poultry were slowly turning on spits above the flames. At the door Madame Bocuse welcomed us. In the old-fashioned pattern of serious French restaurants in those days, the husband was in charge of the kitchen and the wife was in charge of the dining room. I remember her in an elegant white boucle suit, her blonde hair swept up into a thick chignon. She was warm but also dignified in a manner the French carry off to perfection. She knew already that we would be dining chez Bocuse for two nights—a sign of serious eaters.

We took our time studying the menu, again a simple two-page *carte* listing à la carte selections on one side and two set menus on the other. Like the Troisgros menu, the Bocuse menu I still have is covered with Peter's large scrawl, noting what we had the first night and what he proposed for the second. I can see that for the first meal I had *Terrine de foie gras frais des Landes* (fresh foie gras), then *Rables de lièvre à la crème* (a saddle of hare in cream) and *Crepes à l'orange* for dessert. Peter appears to have had three courses plus dessert on the first night, an awesome extravagance: *Rouget poche—sauce au pistou* (poached fish), then *Mousse de truite à la Constant Guillot*, and finally the *Rables de lièvre à la crème* along with me. And the crepes! Perfection, all of it.

The second night is a haze but the menu tells me that I began with *Croustade de truffes au foie gras* (I *love* foie gras) and that we both had *Perdrix aux choux*, tiny birds with delicate cabbage. What I remember most about that dish was the tiny paté made with the teeny-tiny liver of the teeny-tiny birds. It was almost too "precious" to bear but so delicious that we could overlook the extreme.

By the time we'd made our way back to Paris, we had had a surfeit of fabulous dishes. In a moment of amused insanity, we decided to rate them all on a scale of one to five, with one being the most delicious. Our levels were one: transcendental; two: excellent; three: very good; four: mediocre; and five: stinky—hardly scientific but definitely reflective of our feelings. With our collection of menus and our memories of each and every dish, we rated Barrier, Troisgros, Bocuse, and two others: Père Bise in Talloires, and Mère Brazier in Lyons. Not surprisingly, the top restaurant in our pantheon was Troisgros, with a score of 1.5. How we arrived at these decimals is beyond me at this point, but what I love is the list rating every dish we had. Like everything else about that trip, it was excessive but wonderful.

Before we set out for the final act of The Wedding Special—our three weeks in Morocco—there was just one more over-the-top meal . . . the cheese binge. Paris is a city that abounds in delicious cheeses and in the 1970s Androuet was *the* cheese emporium in all Paris. On the street level was a shop that sold hundreds of different cheeses as well as cheese "accoutrements"—from bread to knives to straw serving platters. Upstairs was a restaurant that specialized—of course—in dishes based on cheese: fondues and quiches and cheese soups and croque monsieurs and cheese desserts.

So Peter had something unique in mind for our last Parisian meal on that trip. In any French restaurant, it was possible to order *les fromages*—the cheese course. But at Androuet *les fromages* was not one platter or cart with five to ten cheeses. No, no. At Androuet *les fromages* entailed a selection of something like 150 different cheeses, perhaps even more in "the high season." Who knew that there are seasons for cheese, but there are. Of course, no one could sample all of them, and certainly not as the traditional cheese course after a full meal. So Peter ordered for us an enormous salad of lettuce and tomato and *les fromages.* I remember that the waiter looked

quite skeptical. Did we really not want an *entrée?* No *plat principal?* "*Non,*" Peter said firmly. "*Nous voulons une salade tomate énorme et les fromage, tout les fromages.*"

The parade of cheese began immediately, starting with the most mild and working up to the most strong, each category of cheeses brought on its own straw platter. The first offering was soft, mild cheeses like ricotta and feta. We pointed out to the waiter which we'd like, and he served us small pieces of each we'd selected. Soon another platter arrived, with seven to ten cheeses of the different type—perhaps hard mild cheeses like aged Dutch Gouda or manchego. Another platter held a selection of about ten different blue cheeses, from *Bleu de Gex* to Roquefort to Gorgonzola. It went on and on as we were fascinated to compare the nuances of flavor in multiple cheeses in the same grouping. Much red wine accompanied this exercise, of course, so one could refresh one's palate between those nuances of flavor. A *lot* of palate refreshing took place over the several hours of that meal.

By the time we had worked our way up to the final platter—really stinky cheeses like Limburger—I was almost catatonic. Not that I had sampled 150 cheeses, but it felt as though I had. When we staggered out of Androuet that night, neither Peter nor I ever wanted to see cheese again. Of course, it helped that we were going to Morocco the next day—a cuisine where cheese plays no role at all. Still, the excess of that last meal was somehow fitting for the three-star extravaganza we had spent the last few weeks indulging ourselves in!

Côte de Boeuf au Fleurie

One Christmas after this extravaganza, Elinor gave Peter the cookbook *les recettes originales de Jean et Pierre Troisgros, Cuisineirs à Roanne.* Here are the recipes for the divine *Côte de boeuf au Fleurie* that I had the first night in Roanne.

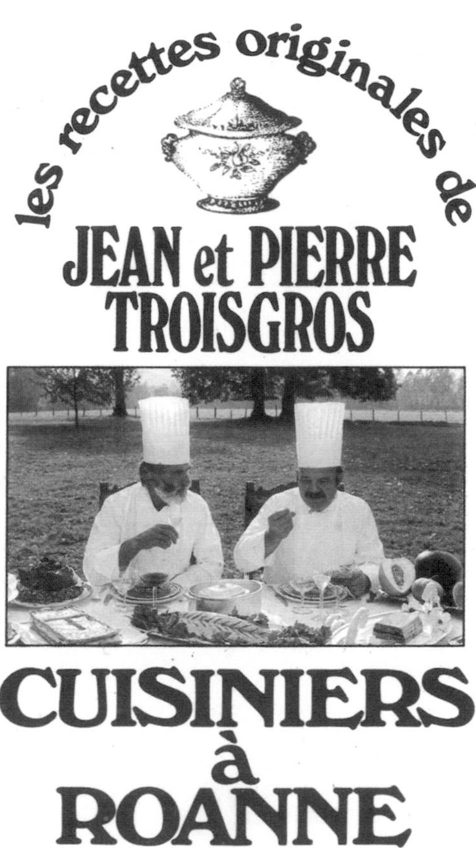

côte de bœuf au Fleurie

Temps de préparation : 30 minutes
Temps de cuisson : 30 minutes

Ingrédients pour 4 personnes
1 côte de bœuf parée de 1,300 kg
25 cl de Fleurie
2 échalotes grises
120 g de moelle
180 g de beurre
4 noix de glace de viande (*voir recette p. 34*)
Sel, poivre

MISE EN PLACE :

1. *Le bœuf :* Demander au boucher de parer une pièce prise entre la 2e et la 3e côte et de faire le manche, c'est-à-dire mettre l'os à vif.

2. *La moelle :* Se procurer la veille des canons de moelle et les dégorger à l'eau froide pendant 12 heures.

3. Hacher finement l'échalote.

CUISSON :

● Assaisonner la côte de bœuf de sel et poivre, la mettre à cuire dans une sauteuse en cuivre étamé dans laquelle on a amené 40 g de beurre à couleur noisette.

● Laisser cuire environ 15 minutes sur chaque face en arrosant souvent à l'aide d'une cuillère.

● La *réserver* sur un plat où l'on a retourné une assiette afin que la viande ne baigne pas dans le jus qu'elle va rendre.

● Le temps de cuisson est calculé en fonction du temps de repos de la côte qu'il faut prévoir d'au moins 20 minutes dans un endroit tempéré.

● Pendant cette opération, **pocher** la moelle : dans une petite casserole couper les tranches d'un centimètre d'épaisseur et les recouvrir d'eau froide salée. Chauffer lentement jusqu'à ébullition et retirer du feu.

LA SAUCE :

Verser la graisse de cuisson dans une poêle, mettre l'échalote hachée à l'intérieur de la sauteuse et la laisser légèrement **suer. Déglacer** avec le vin rouge, ajouter alors la glace de viande et laisser réduire d'une bonne moitié.
Retirer la sauteuse et ajouter par petits morceaux le beurre en fouettant lentement pour l'incorporer.
La maintenir à 70°, la sauce à ce stade ne devant plus bouillir.
En dépassant cette température la sauce tournerait et il faudrait avoir recours à l'eau froide pour la remonter.
Rectifier l'assaisonnement et passer au chinois fin.

DRESSAGE :

Réchauffer la côte dans la poêle avec le beurre de cuisson. La dresser sur un plat de service et la **napper** de sauce au Fleurie dans laquelle on incorpore le jus rendu par la viande au repos.
Égoutter la moelle sur une serviette et la déposer délicatement sur la côte.
Découper la viande en 8 tranches parallèles à l'os et servir en garniture du gratin forézien (*voir recette p. 288*).

Glace de Viande

glace de viande

On l'obtient par la réduction du fond de veau brun.

PRÉPARATION :

- Laisser **réduire** le fond à petit feu. A l'aide d'une louche, retirer soigneusement le dépôt qui se forme sur le bord de la casserole. La limpidité de la glace dépend de cette opération.

- Lorsque la réduction avance, transvaser le liquide dans une casserole plus adaptée à la quantité.

- Le liquide doit **réduire** de 9/10, la glace prête doit être limpide, sirupeuse, brillante. Pour ces raisons, la quantité de départ doit être au moins de 4 litres *.

- La glace de viande s'emploie dans la confection du steak au poivre et pour renforcer les sauces.

* Le temps de réduction étant variable selon le bouillonnement, il est impossible de donner un temps précis.

THE GREAT VINEGAR CAPER

Once, we planned an entire trip around vinegar.

In 1976, realizing that this might be the last time the three teenaged Buckleys would willingly endure a family trip, I organized a summer in Europe for the five of us—thanks to the three-hundred-dollar charter flight tickets I managed to book.

Peter was the consummate planner. In truth, his idea of the perfect trip would have been to take off with no fixed plans and all the time (and money) in the world. But neither time nor money were limitless, jet planes had changed the hotel capacities of Europe forever, and we were a band of five. All of these factors threw Peter in heavy Planning Mode long before our July departure date. Of course, I was part of the planning, voicing my opinion, making suggestions, but in most cases I was delighted to let the expert plot a course for my consideration, always feeling lucky that we had our own Cook's Tour director in residence.

Watching Peter plan a trip was part of the joy of traveling with Peter. Seeing a master at his craft, setting out his utensils, gathering his resources, preparing his ingredients. Out came the maps and the books. Memories of places loved and savored, places and people he wanted to share with us. And of course, inspirations of food to be found in one corner of the world or another.

Before our 1976 trip, Peter and I had become completely enamored with the two erudite and informative tomes by Waverley Root—*The Food of France* and *The Food of Italy*. As was his wont, Peter devoured *The Food of France* from cover to cover, reading aloud to me wonderful descriptions of the domain of butter, the domain of fat (i.e., lard), and the domain of oil, as Mr. Root divided all French cooking. We drooled over accounts of the perfect way to prepare cassoulet and adored the humanity of the battles that rocked Marseilles housewives and chefs alike: what are the proper and only fish to use in a correctly made bouillabaisse (a subject on which there is clearly as little agreement as on gumbo in my native Louisiana). *The Food of Italy* we read aloud to one another, with frequent digressions by Peter to share with me his own rich lore of Italian eating stories.

So, in the winter and spring of 1976, Waverley Root played a large role in "The Planning." Through a good friend who had worked with Mr. Root in the legendary days of the *Paris Tribune*, Peter contacted Root by mail. In return, he received the first of several letters, charming, gracious, and dotted with little tidbits of culinary lore, and an invitation to visit when in Paris. With the books and the letters, Peter added and subtracted stops and routes for our peregrinations.

So for this trip, our chief Rootian Grail was vinegar—balsamic vinegar, to be exact. Today, while the local supermarket offers an assortment of balsamic vinegars and unsophisticated cooks sprinkle it on everything every day, it is hard to imagine that in 1976 there may not have been a bottle to be found in the United States. Peter, supremely well-educated and well-experienced in food, had heard of it but never tasted it.

Waverley Root recounted stories of how the brave residents of the northern Italian city of Modena—ground zero for balsamic vinegar—carried their precious kegs of the vinegar out of the city strapped to the backs of their bicycles as they fled Allied bombs in World War II. That they chose vinegar over all other possessions was a telling testament to the value of this mystical liquid.

Peter suggested that a trip to Modena was called for. I happily concurred. The fact that Modena had other claims to fame—Luciano Pavarotti and Ferraris, for example—paled in comparison to the eating possibilities, for of course there was more for the mouth than the mysterious vinegar. The restaurant Fini was cited by Waverley Root as an outstanding place to savor the culinary delights of the province of Emilia-Romagna.

With extensive mouth-watering, we contemplated the possibilities of *bollito misto* and the world's best tortellini.

So, as part of The Last Great Family Trip to Europe, we found ourselves pulling up in front of the Fini Hotel in Modena one very hot July day in 1976. There were just three of us. Annabel was off in Provence for the first of three summers, and David was en route to family friends on the Côte d'Azur. Peter's mother, Elinor, was ensconced in her beloved Venice, where she had just treated us to two weeks of bliss. But Michael, Peter, and I had come to find the famed vinegar of Modena.

In 1976 the Fini Hotel was just on the edge of change. The hotel itself was a hybrid, part old-fashioned Italian-small-city hotel with courtly service and creaky elevators, part new Italian modern, a bit cold and chrome. Attached were the famous

Fini Restaurant and a small shop, even then marketing the Fini products one can now order on the Internet.

When we arrived, Peter, at home with the ways of European hotels since infancy, had a chat with the concierge, the source of all wisdom, information, and success in such establishments. In those days, the Fini was old-fashioned enough to have a real concierge, not the brisk and impersonal "help desks" or even colder computer information systems too many hotels have today. But this was another age, so in the time-honored fashion, Peter let the Fini concierge know that we were in the market for some very good Modena vinegar. The elegant man with luxuriant mustache and the concierge's badge of crossed keys first directed us to the small shop. But, he allowed, he might also be able to locate for us some private purveyors of older, rarer vintages. People might be in touch, he said, leaving us not quite sure whether this would be something official or clandestine. It would be the latter.

We three piggy Buckleys passed several happy days in Modena, much of which involved food—exquisite food. Meanwhile, however, The Great Vinegar Caper mounted in intensity. Several times a day, at unexpected hours, a conspiratorial knock would sound at the door—always a light, rather secretive set of knocks. Upon opening the door, we would find a Modenese man, usually dressed in a white shirt and black pants, usually looking intense and a bit furtive (though that may have been our intrigued imaginations at work). "*Andiamo*," Peter would say, and in the man would slither.

Of the Italian negotiation that ensued, I was a fascinated spectator. Though my Italian was almost nonexistent, the small but universal theater piece unfolding before me needed no translation. Our guest always began by welcoming us to his city and then allowed that he had word that we were in the market for some *very* special examples of its famed vinegar. And he of course could provide just such. The age of the vinegar was always of first importance, produced like a gift: fifty-year-old Modena vinegar made a year after Peter was born, eighty-year-old Modena vinegar, even one flask of one-hundred-year-old vinegar. The prices of this vinegar were commensurately rarified. In embarking on this search, we had had no idea of the value of truly old Modena vinegar. Even the very, very best sherry vinegar we could buy at Fauchon in Paris then cost an unheard of twenty-five dollars a bottle. Now we were being offered small flasks of vinegar for hundreds of dollars. Hundreds of 1976 dollars. After the first visitor quoted a price, Peter and I had agreed that we probably had set out after an unaffordable Grail. But Peter treated each of the Vinegar Ambassadors with his due dignity, showed the proper respect for the undoubted superiority of his offering, and proposed to contact him later once we had made our decision. Everyone shook hands, said *arrivederci*, and the vinegar man slipped out as quietly as he'd entered. And a few hours later, another character out of *James Bond* lightly tapped at our door.

Eventually we took the only rational course (something we weren't always known for doing when it came to food) and bought several expensive but not insane bottles of balsamic vinegar at the Fini shop. One of those bottles we gave Jean Troisgros when we saw him a few days later. Astonishingly now, Troisgros had never heard of, much less tasted or used, balsamic vinegar. He was thrilled to receive it, immediately opening the bottle to take a small swig. Pronouncing it *très interessant*, he gave us in exchange a bottle of the incredible vinegar that good French chefs make out of the wine left in bottles returned from the dining room.

Over the next few years Peter played with balsamic vinegar. He used it judiciously, inventively, and usually deliciously—to glaze pork, to caramelize onions, to flavor strawberries, and sometimes for a special salad. Then, as cheap versions of balsamic vinegar became the ubiquitous staple of American kitchens, Peter lost interest in what became a much overused flavor.

Still, whenever anyone asked if we liked balsamic vinegar, we smiled conspiratorially and remembered: "*Signore, volete comprare un po' di aceto? Di aceto* molto *vecchio?*" "Sir, would you like to buy a little vinegar? *Very old* vinegar?"

Beef Nancy

The balsamic vinegar we first brought back from Italy was far too precious to cook with, but once balsamic became readily available in the corner store, Peter occasionally used it in a dish. Mostly, though, we preferred it on plain lettuce with some excellent olive oil. Here is one of Peter's inventions using good quality—though not insanely expensive—Modena vinegar.

5 lbs. beef roast (chuck, bottom round, or rump)
¾ cup Modena vinegar
2 cups good quality beef broth, preferably homemade*
3 Tbsp. tomato paste
¼ lb. slab bacon
2 medium-size onions
2 cups chopped sweet peppers (mix of red and yellow—approximately 4 peppers)
Olive oil, as needed
Black pepper and salt to taste
1 cup red wine
Egg noodles

Marinate meat in vinegar, beef broth, and tomato paste for 6 hours or overnight. Bring to room temperature.

Cook bacon over low heat to render fat until bacon is crisp. Remove bacon from pan with slotted spoon.

Sauté onions and peppers in bacon fat until soft but not brown (adding a bit of olive oil if necessary). Add a pinch of salt. Add red wine and reduce the liquid by half.

Starting with meat and marinade at room temperature, add to the red wine, pepper, and onion mixture in a Dutch oven. Bring to a low boil on top of stove, and then place in a

350°F oven. Cook for 3 hours, reducing oven temperature to keep liquid no higher than a simmer. (It is important not to let the liquid boil, which will toughen the meat!**) Adjust seasonings as necessary.

Serve over egg noodles.

*Peter used 2 Tbsp. Bovril dissolved in 2 cups of boiling water, but Bovril is hard to find. Using 2 Tbsp. freeze-dried miso dissolved in 2 cups of boiling water is another alternative.

**In his charming and unusual cookbook *Feasts for All Seasons*, Roy Andries de Groot says, "It is impossible to be a good cook without understanding precisely what is meant by 'simmering.' . . . True simmering avoids all bubbling by keeping the water just below the boiling temperature. Even the gentlest bubbling is not true simmering. How then, is one to know that the water remains very close to boiling? Fortunately, there is a visible sign. When the water is just, just below boiling, the surface slowly moves, to and fro, round and about, as if crisscrossed by tiny currents. The French have a wonderfully descriptive term for it. They say that the water is *riant*, which means 'smiling.'"

Chicken in Vinegar and Cider

Peter loved vinegar, all kinds of vinegar. Often, he flavored vinegar himself, with everything from hot peppers to herbs.

8 chicken thighs
2 Tbsp. olive oil
2 Tbsp. butter
6 slices thick-cut bacon
1 large onion, chopped
2 sweet Italian green peppers, chopped
Scant cup of hot pepper vinegar
Scant cup of fresh apple cider
Spinach

To make hot pepper vinegar:

Place sliced jalapeño pepper, with seeds, in a scant cup of good cider vinegar. Allow pepper to marinate for at least 2 hours; then remove pepper pieces including seeds.

Cook bacon and allow to cool so that it can be crumbled. Reserve 1 Tbsp. bacon fat.

Brown chicken pieces in a Dutch oven with oil, butter, and some of the bacon fat. Remove chicken and sauté chopped onion and sweet peppers in remaining fat. Return chicken to pan, with crumbled bacon. (This can be done ahead of time.) Add pepper vinegar and cider and bring to a simmer. Place in a 375°F oven and cook for about 35–40 minutes until chicken is cooked through.

Serve on a bed of hot, fresh spinach. Polenta is the perfect accompaniment.

WHEN THE KILLERS CAME TO TOWN

"Ham and lima beans for dinner!" Peter would periodically announce.

This always meant Antonio was in town. The matador Antonio Ordóñez was one of Peter's best friends. A man who could afford anything he wanted for dinner, anywhere in the world, Antonio adored Birds Eye frozen lima beans. And like all Spaniards, he seemed to want to eat ham for breakfast, lunch, and dinner. Antonio was used to getting what he wanted, and at our house what he always wanted was ham and lima beans.

Peter and Antonio had become friends in Spain in 1950, when Antonio was eighteen and Peter was twenty-five. Antonio was then the rising star of the bull ring and the favorite of Ernest Hemingway, who was in those days a looming presence in the bullfight world. Antonio and his brother-in-law, Luis Miguel Dominguín, would be the center of *The Dangerous Summer*, the book Hemingway wrote about the 1959 bullfight season and the rivalry between the two bullring superstars.

A few winters after Peter and I were married, Antonio and his family swept into town. He'd come with his wife, Carmen, their two grown daughters, Carmencita and Belén, and Belén's fiancé, whose name I have long forgotten (the marriage was brief). Purpose of the trip: buying sheets for Belén's trousseau. In short order the ham-and-lima-bean dinner was arranged, and on the appointed evening they arrived at our door.

I'd never met "the Killers," as Peter called them (*matador* being the Spanish word for "killer"), and the children hadn't seen them for years. We were all dressed up, and so was the table, candles flickering, silver and crystal glittering. The ham was in the oven and the lima beans were ready. No elaborate bean dishes for Antonio, just simple lima beans with lots of butter and salt and pepper. As always, Peter was the chief cook, though I was more than the bottle washer as I'd made an apple pie for this prototypical American dinner. This was early in our marriage and I was heavily into my fruit pie period. (Early on Peter had declared that fruit tarts were his favorite dessert, so I set out to become the fruit tart specialist.)

When the doorbell rang, twelve-year-old Annabel went to do the honors. I heard the door open and Antonio's wonderful deep voice: "*Hola*, Annabel." Then, dead silence. What in the world was going on? At the door I found Annabel staring, speechless, at a vision of white fur that seemed to fill the entire hallway. Greater quantities of white fur on more incredibly beautiful women than either of us had ever seen: the gorgeous and glamorous Carmen in white mink, Carmencita in white fox, and Belén in white ermine—all just purchased at Saks (clearly more than sheets were on the shopping list). It took your breath away—as it had Annabel's.

Soon Peter was there, and a mad crush of *abrazos* ensued as Antonio and Peter pounded one another on the back, as Peter embraced Carmen, whom he adored, and warmly welcomed the girls and the now-nameless fiancé. Spanish was flowing around us as I suggested to Annabel that she take the fur coats to the bedroom, which I knew she was dying to do. Everyone got settled and drink orders were taken when I realized that Annabel had not returned from her mission. Tiptoeing to the bedroom door, I opened it quietly and beheld a delicious sight: Annabel, spinning around the room, completely wrapped in white fur.

White fur was only part of the glamour when the Killers came to town. Their visits always involved Mary Hemingway, a key part of the world they'd all shared in Spain in the late 1950s. It was a time when young Americans like Peter and Brits like Ken Tynan hung around the bullrings. Pretty soon,

Peter started filming the bullfights and getting to know the men who fought them. Bullfighting is all about movement—men, bulls, capes, swords. It's all about making the right and most graceful moves at the perfect time. At some point, though, in a paradoxical reversal, Peter moved from filming the action with a movie camera to capturing the action with a still camera. Something about freezing a single moment was more dramatic and more challenging to him. When he showed his bullfight photographs to Dick Simon at Simon & Schuster, he soon had a book contract for the book he called *Bullfight.* As he worked on the book in the late 1950s, Peter traveled across Spain with Antonio and others for one bullfight season after another; from Cordoba, to Madrid, to Barcelona, to Nimes, and back to Seville on the circuit from April to September.

It was in those years that Peter got to know Ernest Hemingway on his own. He'd known Hemingway as a child in Paris. Now, twenty years later, Peter was part of that other movable feast, the bullfight aficionados who moved from feria to feria across Spain. At the center of this international group was "the great American writer." Hemingway was increasingly irascible and unpredictable by then, well on his way to ending his life with a shotgun, and Peter's relationship with him veered from a warm "Mister Papa" father/son intimacy to a prickly "who do you think you are, young man" standoff when Ernest felt that Peter was intruding on his "ownership" of the bullfight world or his relationship with Antonio. But Mary was always Peter's friend.

By the time I came on the scene, Ernest was long dead, though for years I felt as though he were a character in our lives as Peter worked on his Hemingway biography, *Ernest,* published in 1978. Peter's desk was constantly covered with photographs of Ernest from infancy to his death, books on Cuba, Peter's notes on his trip to Oak Park, manuscript written as always on yellow legal pads with black Flair pens. I felt as though I was on a first-name basis with Papa himself. There were endless calls with the network of Hemingway friends, stories exchanged, letters unearthed from old files, and visits from Jack and Patrick Hemingway as well as Jack's three daughters—Joan, Margaux, and Mariel.

It was around this time that Margaux, then a glamorous supermodel, decided that she was going to make a movie and that Peter would be in it. Sadly, in the end there was no movie, but it did lead to the creation of Peter's unforgettable stage name. One morning I overheard Peter saying, "Boulder, Boulder Congo," with a certain panache. When I enquired about just what he was talking about, Peter said with a twinkle, "Well, Rock Hudson was a movie star, but a rock is pretty small. And, really, the Hudson is not a very prepossessing river. I need a better name than that. I like Boulder Congo! What do you think?" I was speechless.

Meanwhile, we saw Mary all the time. When the Killers were here, however, the glamour factor was ratcheted up by ten. Antonio loved to go out, so night after night a parade of black limos picked us up for what could only be called "a night on the town." Totally unlike our ordinary life, we went to grand restaurants with posh people, all part of the movie-star world that surrounded a bullfighter like Antonio. One typical evening started out at the NBC studios where a producer interviewed Antonio and Mary. Next we traipsed off to one of the old-fashioned French restaurants like La Caravelle that Mary loved. In the warm peachy light that seemed to suffuse all of those dining rooms (lit to show off the clientele and the flowers to best advantage), a maître d'hotel attended to the Widow Hemingway's every request with just the right balance of formality, dignity, and obsequiousness. After a classical dinner of something like blanquette de veau, we were on to the next round, picking up the heiress Christina Heeren, whose father had been a great friend of Antonio's, and off to El Morocco then in one of its periodic zebra-striped reincarnations, this time as a private club. While Christina glided from one table to another, greeting society friends, I could just imagine Ernest in black-and-white sitting at a booth looking like the famous photographs of him there with Marlene Dietrich.

Even walking down the street with Antonio and his family was like being with movie stars. Who knew there were so many Spanish tourists in Manhattan, but every one of them wanted to shake Antonio's hand. "*Maestro*," they would say, the men bowing slightly to the matador. Carmen herself was bullfight royalty. Her father and generations before him were famous matadors. Her brother was the superstar Luis Miguel Dominguín. Her husband was Antonio. And her daughter Carmencita was married to Paquirri, a rising young matador who would later be killed in the ring.

Then in 1982 Carmen died of cancer, and for a while there were no more announcements of "ham and lima beans." I wanted to go to Spain to see Antonio, but Peter couldn't bring himself to do it. The idea that "you can't go back" was too deeply engrained in his psyche. Since the fifties, he'd gone back to Spain only once, in 1968, when he accompanied Mary to Pamplona for the dedication of a statue of Ernest. In Peter's eyes, too much about Spain had changed, and not for the better. Not that he was a Franco admirer—far from it—but between 1950 and the 1980s, Spain had entered the modern world (as of course it had to). In those years, the Europe that Peter knew and loved in his childhood and young adulthood changed irrevocably. Peter had crisscrossed Spain when there were almost no other cars. In his Spain he once left his camera bag sitting on the hood of his car and came back to find a man guarding it. Now, he knew, pickpocketing was rampant. In his Spain, the Costa del Sol was a quiet and beautiful coastline. Now it was lined with high-rise hotels filled with tourists who arrived on nonstop flights from England and Germany. So no, Peter said, he did not want to go back to Spain, not even to see Antonio.

In the mid-1980s, though, Peter had a reason to go. His biography *Ernest* was published by Dial Press in 1978, and any time Peter's name was linked with Hemingway's, bullfighting and Antonio inevitably came to the fore. There was a brief—and ultimately elusive—plan to make a movie based on *Ernest*. So Peter stopped in Madrid to see Antonio on his way home from scouting locations in Italy. Sitting in the lobby of the Ritz, he heard the familiar deep voice behind him: *"Hola, Chiquitin!"* and there was Antonio. With him was a lovely woman looking both puzzled and amazed. *Chiquitin* means "the wee one," and Antonio had prepared her for meeting a small, shy American friend. As Peter unfolded his large, six-foot-four-inch body from the chair, the woman began to laugh. This was Pilar, Antonio's second wife (Antonio, a man who could not be without a wife, had remarried soon after

Carmen's death). A lively, handsome redhead, Pilar was totally different from the glamorous Carmen. She had made a career as a civil servant and had nothing to do with the bullfight world, but she loved Antonio, and that was all that mattered.

Pilar also loved New York, so soon she and Antonio began coming once a year around Christmastime. Pilar came from a very different world than Carmen had. Gone were the days of Mary and limos and white fur coats and El Morocco, but in their place were years of warm, happy, companionable friendship. And since Pilar spoke English quite well, I was relieved of the stress of either silence—never my first choice—or stumbling along in my pathetic Spanish. We'd had a succession of Latin American housekeepers, so my "domestic" Spanish was excellent. I could chatter away with words like *planchar* (to iron), *limpiar* (to clean), *aspiradora* (the vacuum cleaner). But a discussion on the virtues of American versus Spanish politics or the merits of one bullfighter over another was quite out of the question.

Soon Pilar was urging us to visit them, so at last, in 1988, we planned a trip. We'd stop in Ronda, where Antonio was born; stay with them in Seville; then make a road trip on our own to Cádiz and Granada.

From the moment we landed in Malaga and drove to Ronda, I was entranced. Southern Spain felt different from the France and Italy I knew so well. White villages dotted the dry, scrubby hills as we drove north. When we reached Ronda, we went right away to Antonio's finca (farm). Pilar had the flu in Seville. So we were left to our own devices for a few days in beautiful Ronda. Always one for a dramatic entrance, Peter took me first to the astonishing chasm, El Tajo, which dominates the town. As we stood on the bridge over the gorge, he reveled in telling me perhaps true, perhaps apocryphal tales of people thrown off it in days past. With that in mind, the bullring seemed tame in comparison.

Modern bullfighting began in Ronda in the eighteenth century, and all of the narrow cobbled streets in the old town seemed to lead to the bullring, said to be the oldest in Spain. Antonio was everywhere in evidence. Not only did he own the bullring, but the shops were filled with pictures of him in the ring and with celebrities—chiefly, Ernest Hemingway and Orson Welles. Why Orson Welles, we wondered? Then we found out: Wandering around the yard at the finca one afternoon, I stopped to read the plaque on the pretty well set in front of the house. The inscription said the ashes of Orson Welles were buried in that very well. It turned out that Welles, a close friend and an admirer of Antonio, had spent a lot of time in Ronda and wanted his ashes scattered at the finca. What could be more appropriate than in a well? We called it Orson's well, of course.

After a few days Antonio arrived to take us to Seville. On the way, he said, we had to stop at one of the two ranches where he raised fighting bulls, so he could "try out" a young matador he'd decided to manage. Antonio had retired from the ring, but his entire life had been and always would be totally and completely focused on *los toros*. For Antonio, it was all bulls all the time.

Today, the bullfight is such a foreign and horrifying concept to most Americans that it is hard to explain why and how it could be totally compelling. Peter used to say that it was impossible to predict how someone would respond. Some, sure they would like it, couldn't bear it. Others, sure they'd hate it, loved it.

I'd seen my first bullfight in France in the 1980s when we were staying near Arles at the time of the September feria (a series of bullfights put on every day for about a week). Peter chose a day when there were "good" matadors, men whose names he'd heard from Antonio. I was nervous, as I wanted desperately to like it, knowing how important the bullfight was to Peter. He'd spent years in that world and he'd written a highly acclaimed book about it. But I love animals. How could I watch a bull being killed in front of me?

Sitting in the Roman arena in Arles, where the feria was held, I was nervous, excited, fascinated by the fact that I was in an ancient arena where gladiators had fought, about to watch something so foreign but so intriguing. I'd read *Death in the Afternoon* and *The Sun Also Rises* and Peter's book of course. But I knew I wasn't prepared for the real thing. Then the spectacle began. The men paraded into the arena, the matadors in their gorgeous "suits of light," the cuadrilla on horseback, the crowd roaring.

I cannot begin to describe a bullfight. Others have done far too a good a job for me to write even one more sentence picturing it. Now I find bullfighting indefensible—which makes it even harder to write about—but for a few years when I first saw it, I was electrified. Hemingway nailed it when he said that its fascination was all about death. The fact that the matador slips past death—real death, not just danger—every time he executes a graceful pass gives the event a drama that nothing else has—at least nothing else that you can sit and watch in a sunlit arena in the late afternoon.

So by the time Antonio picked us up that day in Ronda, I had seen a number of bullfights. Thanks heavens, for I was about to see one from a very, very, *very* close vantage point! Pilar had driven out from Seville to meet us, and in short order we were sitting in a tiny arcaded area right alongside the small ring. And I mean *right* alongside. This was bullfighting "up close and personal." Only a concrete barrier around the ring, about twelve inches thick, separated us from the gargantuan animal that soon roared into the ring. Of course there was nothing between the young matador and the bull except a pink and yellow silk cape, but still, my own closeness felt breathtaking. We watched as the matador turned the bull with a sweep of the cape, over and over, with Antonio calling out directions that I couldn't understand. As the bull pounded past me, twelve inches away, I just kept thinking, "Thank God I have seen this before!"

At last it was over, and the men came into the ring to drag the enormous, very dead animal out. Peter and Antonio went to join them. "Come," Peter said, but I refused, "No, no, I *cannot* watch them butcher the bull." I was adamant. So was Peter. "You eat beef, right? Lots of it?" I conceded the point. "If you can't watch where it comes from, you shouldn't eat it," he tossed over his shoulder as he strode off.

So, reluctantly, I followed the men and the bull out into the courtyard where a team of butchers waited. And I watched as the once massive animal was turned into meat. At first I was highly uncomfortable, watching the animal that had so recently been so vibrantly alive now like a mountain of black flesh being carved up. But I do eat meat and I do live near old-fashioned butcher shops where huge sides of beef hang in the window. Pretty soon, the animal didn't seem like an animal anymore. It had become meat. At least I didn't know its name, I thought.

That evening, our first in Seville, we ate at home, a meal prepared by Antonio and Pilar's cook, Maria, and served by her husband, Manolo. I only remember one dish from that meal. When it was time for the main course, Manolo, wearing white gloves, entered the dining room with a large silver platter. Resplendent on a plate in the center of the platter were what I instantly knew to be . . . the bull's balls. Peter and Antonio thought this was hilariously funny. Not to be outdone, I didn't miss a beat. I smiled at Manolo as he offered to serve me a slice. "*Muchas gracias*," I said, and proceeded to eat my serving, remembering that Rocky Mountain Oysters really were something people ate and so could I! In fact, the bite tasted fine—sautéed and meaty—but still. . . .

We spent a beautiful week in Seville with Antonio and Pilar. It was springtime and the orange blossoms perfumed the city. We wandered through the Jewish quarter, sat in cafés, went to cathedrals and palaces with the ghosts of Ferdinand and Isabella and Columbus, and one day Peter had a haircut. Sitting in the barber's chair, he looked up at me with a twinkle, "Susan, guess where we are. It's the barber of Seville!"

And of course, we went to bullfights. We'd timed our visit specifically for the Feria de Abril, the series of bullfights held the two weeks after Easter each year. Going to a bullfight in Seville was to enter a different world from that Roman arena in

Arles. Spanish aficionados were *very* serious about the corrida, the bullfight. The arena was huge and packed with what seemed like every level of Spanish society. There were workers dressed in casual clothes and fancy women in elegant suits. There were priests in their habits, old people and teenagers. The crowd didn't feel like any crowd I'd ever sat in. Certainly not the crowd at a sporting event—a tennis match or a baseball game. There was something more formal and more intense about it. What they were about to witness was danger—and death.

We sat with Pilar, while Antonio roamed around the parts of the ring where only the insiders could go. There were crowds of men with him, standing in the space between the ring and the seats. Managers, sword handlers, cape holders, hundreds of people attending the star, and the bullfighter himself. I remember thinking how strange it must feel to Antonio, used to being the star himself, now on the edges. Still, though, he was treated with the utmost deference by everyone.

After it was over, we all repaired to a café just across from the arena and there, Antonio was once again the star. Really, it was like being somewhere with Frank Sinatra or Elvis Presley. A constant flow of admirers were streaming past to shake his hand, to seek his opinion, or just to say *hola*.

One night after the bullfight—long after, since of course dining any time before about 10:00 p.m. was considered impossible, uncivilized, probably causing early death—we went out to dinner at an especially elegant place. Either Peter or I innocently ordered gazpacho and pronounced it delicious. Instantly, Antonio and Pilar each requested a taste, and marital discord quickly followed. Just as Provençal cooks talk about bouillabaisse and Louisiana cooks argue about gumbo, gazpacho is the cause of unending dispute. There is absolutely no agreement about what should or should not be in it—except tomatoes as a universal ingredient. (But wait, I stand corrected, for there is a famous "white gazpacho" made with almonds.) Peter and I were soon the bemused audience for what we dubbed The Great Gazpacho Contest. The next day both Pilar and Antonio could be seen in the kitchen, animatedly giving Maria dircctions as she diplomatically nodded to each of them. And sure enough that evening, Manolo appeared in the dining room, white gloves and all, with first one and then another large tureen of gazpacho. Pilar's was thick and pure, with a gorgeous taste of olive oil and tomatoes, nothing more. Antonio's version, on the other hand, was thinner, still delicious, but with assorted things floating in it—from pieces of cucumber and celery, to halves of hardboiled egg. This, he pronounced, is how his mother made it (clearly the gold standard in his eyes).

I wish I could remember just what Peter and I said as we very gingerly navigated these perilous shoals. Just which

version of gazpacho did we prefer? In fact, we both preferred Pilar's, but what in the world did Peter say that left the Maestro himself with his ego intact?! I retreated to smiling and saying "Mmmm good" like a little Campbell's soup girl. Peter somehow figured out something, as all were friends when we arose. But it was a delicate moment.

Before we left for Cádiz, there was one more memorable visit, to Antonio's other bull ranch. While Pilar supervised the preparation of an outdoor picnic, Antonio took us on a tour in his Jeep. With Peter by his side and me bouncing along in the back, he drove through the fields thick with wildflowers. With us on a white horse was the mayoral, the ranch foreman, who opened each gate for us to drive through. No walking of course, as each field was the domain of a few bulls that appeared to be lounging about living the life of Ferdinand. Of course they weren't really lounging, but they were peacefully sniffing flowers and eating cork from cork trees. It was Ferdinand reincarnated; lots and lots of Ferdinands. Thinking of the abysmal lives of cattle on American feedlots, I could not help thinking how lucky these animals were in comparison, even knowing what they would face on the one afternoon that would end each of their lives.

After Seville, we left the bullfighters and the bullfighting world. Cádiz was our next stop—a seacoast city totally different in feel from elegant Seville. We ate crispy fried whitebait and drank sherry at restaurants on the beach, dined on the freshest fish every night in an old-fashioned restaurant called El Faro, sampled what seemed like one hundred different kinds of olives in the market, and learned that you should never, ever put your fingers into a vat or jar of olives or they'll spoil.

The sherry was a special revelation. For most of my life, the only sherry I'd been exposed to was sweet New York state sherry. Not as undrinkable as cooking sherry, but almost as bad. When my beloved grandmother—a lifelong teetotaler—was in her eighties, the doctor said, "You know, Mrs. Culpepper, a little sherry before dinner would be good for your circulation." Lo and behold, my Victorian grandmother took to it readily. Small glasses of sherry were served before dinner and even the grandchildren were allowed a glass once we were teenagers. Looking back at it, I realize I would find that sherry totally undrinkable today and it bore absolutely *no* resemblance to anything a Spaniard would bring within a hundred miles of his lips. Under Peter's tutelage, I had expanded my repertoire to Tio Pepe, but I'd never tasted anything like the sherry we drank in Spain—dry and nutty and totally delicious.

It was in Cádiz, watching the waiters at El Faro, that I had my "lightbulb moment" about the difference between the French, the Italians, and the Spanish. Comparison is odious and stereotypes are worse, but to the extent one can generalize, the French really are more intellectual, rational, critical. The Italians really are more open, warm, inhalers of life in all its messy glory. And the Spanish really are the most dignified. They have a certain gravitas, a stature, holding themselves high and proud.

Granada and the Alhambra were our last stop. The Alhambra—just the name sounded romantic, rolling off your tongue in that dangerous way that makes it sound as though you can speak Spanish when you really can't (then what happens when someone answers you?!). And as an avid reader of Washington Irving in my childhood, I was sure it was going to be fabulous, in the true meaning of that word. It was, but not at first, when it was mobbed with wall-to-wall tourists, busload after busload (Peter, who remembered it empty in the 1950s, wouldn't even go in). At this point we were traveling around Granada in a taxi, Antonio having warned us to leave our car at his house where it would not be a tempting target for thieves. Our gregarious driver nodded knowingly when Peter described the Alhambra in the old days. But did you know, he said, that you can visit at night? Sure enough, we returned that night and spent an hour wandering in the vast, silent rooms of the palace, imagining Moors around every corner. Lit by a full moon, it was magical.

After Granada, we went home to New York. It would be ten years before I went back to Spain. Antonio and Pilar came to New York every winter and there were many Christmas and New Year's dinners at our house—without ham and lima beans for those meals, I might point out—where we spent happy times together.

By the end of December 1996, however, Peter's health had deteriorated precipitously, with complications from diabetes. When Antonio and Pilar arrived in New York for their winter visit, they came to the house right away. Somehow Antonio knew he would never see his friend *Chiquitin* again. He had brought a stack of bullfight magazines, and when Peter went to the hospital the next day, New Year's Eve, he took with him a perfect reflection of the man he was: an immense biography of Zola that he was in the middle of reading, Patricia Wells'

Bistro Cooking that I had given him for Christmas, and Antonio's bullfight magazines.

There is a coda to the story. In 1998 I went back to Spain alone—though the spirit of Peter was with me every moment. For years, Antonio had tried to get us to come to the Feria Goyesca, which he had created in Ronda in the 1950s. For two days each September, the feria celebrated Ronda's central role in the history of the bullfight, with the matadors and the cuadrilla dressed in the style of Goya, who had famously painted bullfighters. Peter and I had never gotten to the Goyesca, but when Antonio and Pilar asked me to come the year after Peter died, I said yes.

It was otherworldly from start to finish. When I arrived at the finca, I stepped into a house party that was like something out of *The Sun Also Rises*. Staying at the house along with me were Christina Heeren (she of the earlier El Morocco adventures) and her husband, John, in from Biarritz; another couple, from Bilbao, longtime aficionados; and several others. Every day there were fifteen to twenty people for lunch and more for dinner. I've never eaten so much protein in my life. Aside from the big salads or gazpacho, everything was meat: ham, steak, chops, chorizo—vast quantities of meat. And what an array of people—international friends and multiple generations of Antonio's family, counts and celebrities like Juan Pedro Domecq, of sherry and bull breeding fame (the Domecq fighting bulls were among the most respected in the world), a sophisticated and gracious man who managed, with flawless English, to make me feel perfectly at home.

Everything in Ronda was awash with Goya—women walking around in lacy dresses and mantillas, looking as if they'd stepped off the walls of the Prado, carriages full of Goya-dressed women sweeping around the arena before the corrida, the matadors and their cuadrillas in outfits from Goya paintings (although Picasso supposedly designed Antonio's own suit of lights for one Feria Goyesca). I went each afternoon with *las senoras* while Antonio and his grandson—the rising young matador Francisco Rivera Ordóñez—were busy with the feria itself. It was like going to a corrida with royalty: Pilar, Belén, her daughter Ranita, and Francisco's fiancé Eugenia, the daughter of the Duchess of Alba.

The real royalty arrived the day after the feria ended, however, when the Queen Mother of Spain came to the finca for lunch. A great aficionada herself, the Queen Mother was a longtime admirer of Antonio. This was a formidable occasion, even in Antonio's world. The cooks had been working for days. A table was laid in the front garden (right by Orson's well), loaded with crystal and silver and flowers. Everyone was dressed for an autumn lunch alfresco. I had brought a special dress for the occasion and, more important, a copy of *Bullfight*, which I had signed for the Queen Mother.

At exactly the appointed moment, two large black Bentleys swept into the courtyard. Out leapt a number of men, who proceeded to undo latches on either side of the back of one of the cars. Whomp! The entire back of the car descended as a ramp and out rolled a very old, beautifully dressed woman. It was the Queen Mother, whose arthritis confined her to a wheelchair. The instant the cars arrived, everyone in the house had gathered at the door, standing at attention to greet her.

Antonio was first, and then Eugenia (the Queen Mother's goddaughter). One by one we all made the proper greeting. I think I curtsied in some faint fashion. I know I was told that one did not shake hands with a queen.

With the Queen Mother for lunch were her secretary, a lovely man who had known Peter in his days around the bull-ring, and two ladies in waiting. Lunch was a delicious cold collation: the ubiquitous gazpacho (Pilar's version) and a cold fish salad of some sort. I kept wanting to pinch myself—I, Susan Grace Washburn Buckley, am having lunch in a garden, next to the ashes of Orson Welles, with a former Queen of Spain, with two people actually called "ladies in waiting," with perhaps the greatest matador of the twentieth century, and the future Dutchess of Alba. It was unreal.

When it was time to go, the Queen Mother's chair was pushed through the house to the courtyard, and there was a scene from *Downton Abbey*. All of the servants were lined up formally outside the door. All dressed up in a black suit and white shirt, holding a bouquet of flowers, was the young son of the caretakers. With all of the dignity that only a Spanish ten-year-old could summon up, he stepped forward, bowed, and presented the flowers to the Queen Mother, who accepted them with a gentle smile. Then, whomp, down came the back of the car, in she was rolled, and off they took. And the next morning, I took off, too.

Antonio is gone now, and the bullfight world is disappearing. But in those days, before everything changed, when the Killers came to town or when we went to visit them, life was very glamorous indeed.

Pilar's Gazpacho

The clear winner of The Great Gazpacho Contest.

1 clove garlic
2 pounds of really good tomatoes, the tastiest you can find
1 cup of really good olive oil
1 large piece of good bread, soaked in really good red wine vinegar (preferably sherry vinegar)
Salt to taste

Press garlic in garlic press. Then mix all ingredients thoroughly in blender or food processor.

Peter's Gazpacho

This is how Peter made gazpacho before The Great Gazpacho Contest. It's delicious, too. This is a party recipe, as it makes about 2½ quarts.

1 lb. cucumbers
2½ lbs. flavorful tomatoes
½ lb. green peppers
½ lb. red onions
5 Tbsp. red wine vinegar
1 cup good olive oil
1¼ Tbsp. salt
2 garlic cloves
¼ tsp. chopped hot peppers
2½ cups water

Peel cucumbers, remove hard core of tomatoes, remove seeds and stem from green peppers, and peel onions. Cut all vegetables into large bite-size pieces and place in large bowl. Add vinegar, oil, salt, garlic, hot peppers, and water. Stir and then mix in blender or food processor until smooth. Serve chilled.

This soup is best made a day in advance. It should be well stirred or shaken before serving, very cold. It keeps well for about a week or can be frozen for up to 6 weeks without losing its flavor.

Gazpacho El Faro

This is the recipe for the gazpacho served at El Faro in Cádiz, another variation on the theme.

2-inch-long piece of baguette, crusts discarded
2 cloves garlic
2 tsp. salt
2 Tbsp. sherry vinegar
1 tsp. sugar
2½ lbs. ripe tomatoes, cored and quartered
½ cup mild extra-virgin olive oil
Finely chopped red and green peppers, to garnish

Soak bread in ½ cup of water, then squeeze bread dry and discard the water. (I often use a little more bread than this and moisten it with the vinegar.)

Mash garlic to a paste with salt. Blend garlic paste, bread, vinegar, and sugar.

Chop half of the tomatoes in food processor. Add garlic paste, bread, then add remaining tomatoes, until mixture is chopped very fine. Gradually add the oil with food processor running.

Transfer to a glass or stainless-steel container. Cover and chill for at least 3 hours. Can be kept for up to 2 days. Serve with chopped peppers for garnish.

HAVE SPOON, WILL TRAVEL

The Caribbean stretched out around us forever—deep blue and calm. Nearby floated the small Zodiac boat we'd used to reach this reef. Below, the water wriggled with life below, but on the surface there was nothing else in sight.

Peter, Michael, and I were standing waist deep in the water inside a reef off the coast of British Honduras. (It was British

Honduras then, not Belize—complete with British soldiers in shorts and wool knee socks, ceiling fans, and Graham Greene surely lurking somewhere in a bar.) We'd been snorkeling for about an hour and had come up for air—so to speak. That is, Michael and I had come up for air. Peter had something else in mind altogether.

"Anyone want a bite to eat?" he asked with a twinkle in his voice.

"Yes?" we questioned expectantly, suspecting what was to come.

Ducking back down into the water, Peter emerged with a prickly, round gray orb, covered with short spikes. "Sea urchins!" Michael and I cried. Sure enough, Peter had spotted a cache of sea urchins lurking under a coral outcropping. Contrary to the experiences of city folk who only encounter urchins as *uni* at sushi bars, Michael and I were experienced open-water urchin eaters. We knew that sea urchins can be found in the oceans and seas all over the world. And while some have long and forbidding spines that make picking them up or eating them almost impossible, the white Caribbean urchins are among the more "approachable" urchins. You can even pick them up without a glove on (although the ever-prepared Peter usually snorkeled with at least one glove).

Michael and I waited (im)patiently as Peter prepared the delicacy for eating, gently cracking the bottom of the urchin's carapace and scooping out the salty-sweet roe. One after another, urchins were brought up and consumed. The delicate act of eating a piece of *uni* with chopsticks in a Japanese restaurant was not for us. Even though that *uni* is more flavorful, we all loved the briny taste of urchin roe eaten in the sea itself, dribbling down your chin only to be washed off with a dip into the warm sea water.

Peter had come, as always, completely equipped. All of his bathing suits had pockets in them. (If they didn't come that way, he had me add them, complete with snaps or zippers.) And in the Caribbean, the bathing suits always held a spoon—a spoon to be used for scooping out the thin lining of roe that lines the inside of a sea urchin. After all, who in their right mind would find themselves in a Caribbean moment without a spoon?

We were shortly to find ourselves in a Caribbean moment without enough food, however. It was summertime and the other children were at camp, but Michael was with us. It was to be my first real dive trip, a few weeks in the waters off British Honduras, site of the world's second-longest barrier reef. In those days, British Honduras was a small, hot British colony, far from the fancy resorts of today's Belize. And unlike the hotel-strewn beaches of Belize today, there was only one place to stay, one main outfitter who arranged fishing and dive trips.

I knew I was in for an adventure from the minute we arrived. Somers—general factotum and later to be our boat captain—picked us up at the airport in a long, low-slung Chevrolet from the 1950s and drove us out to a river straight out of *The African Queen*. A small motorboat waited to take us across to the hotel, a process that required many trips, since we had come with the usual Buckley surplus of luggage. We didn't have a lot of clothes, but we had a LOT of equipment:

multiple snorkels, flippers, masks, regulators, spear guns, tools, spoons(!), and other essentials. In those days, there was not a dive shop to be found in British Honduras, so you had to bring extras of everything. Since Peter started out with a lot of baggage—literally and figuratively—doubling up had astounding effects. This was in the old days, however, when airlines could be talked into allowing bags over and above the two-per-person, forty-pounds-per-bag limits. So, heavy laden, the small motorboat plied the river until the three Buckleys and their luggage had reached the camp. Across the river, we were greeted by Mrs. H., a kind, blowsy woman given to saying, "It must be five o'clock somewhere in the world," at odd hours of the afternoon as she cracked open the Gordon's gin.

Within minutes of our arrival, it became apparent that there was a serious bug problem. Many, many, many bugs—some sort of "no-see-ums" of a ferocious, tropical nature. We quickly decided that it was impossible to stay outdoors unless you were underwater. So into the river we jumped, while Mrs. H. directed the assorted staff to toss mangoes to us (since we weren't quite ready for gin). Remember those bathing suit pockets? For mango-eating in rivers, Peter came equipped with a pocketknife. Of course. Mango skin is tough, so it's ever so much nicer if you can peel your mangoes while floating in a river in the jungles of British Honduras, of course. It was all like something out of a Marx Brothers' movie—and absolute heaven.

The object of this trip was diving, however, and after a few days of mango eating, we set out for ten days along the barrier reef, about twenty miles off the coast. We would be six altogether: the three Buckleys; Somers, the captain; Charles, the divemaster; and the cook, whose name I have intentionally forgotten, for reasons that will quickly become apparent. Our boat was a converted Coast Guard boat, very plain but equipped with the essentials from a compressor for filling tanks to a fresh water shower on the stern. All this for one hundred dollars per day, including staff.

The boat also was supposed to be equipped with food, purchased by the cook and loaded on at the camp. We would be at sea, hours from the camp, for ten days. On the morning of our departure, the cook was seen making many trips back and forth between the little boat that crossed the river and our much larger dive boat. He was loading the food on, we were told. More boxes seemed to be going to the little boat than to the big boat, but who were we to question the logistics of setting up this dive trip.

A few days out, however, it became apparent that there was a problem. We had a modicum of vegetables and rice, lots of mangoes and bananas, but almost no protein. After intense interrogation by both Somers and former counterintelligence officer Buckley, the cook confessed that he had sold most of the meat to his friends back on shore.

Needless to say, there was no way that we were going to give up a minute of our glorious time on the reef to go back to get more food. Anyway, we were surrounded by the bounty of the Caribbean: spiny lobsters, grouper, snappers, and other goodies. So every day, Peter and Somers and Charles went "hunting." Spear guns in hand, they shot our dinner. At first it was fun. What could be better than lobster every night? But after a week, I can tell you, we thought if we ever saw another lobster, we would throw up.

At the end of our idyll on the Honduran reefs, hungry but happy, we crossed "the blue"—the deep, deep water between the barrier reef and the mainland—and headed back to the camp. It was the end of our Lobster Period and the beginning of our Conch Period. The cook at the camp, Somers' wonderful wife, did not have a lot to work with. She made conch fritters and conch stew and conch cakes. And then she made that repertoire all over again. If you've never eaten conch, it's the very tough and relatively tasteless meat from the animal that lives in a conch shell—a bit like abalone.

There were other things besides food to entertain us back on land, however. As we prepared to leave British Honduras, a rollicking group of filmmakers arrived on the scene. Documentary filmmaker Stan Waterman and his crew had come to the camp to shoot underwater footage of sharks out on the reef. Fresh from filming the fabulous great white shark movie, *Blue Water, White Death*, Stan was something of a celebrity, a witty, lively, handsome man who was an underwater pro. In short order, the hotel tables were covered with fascinating underwater camera gear, and he and Peter were trading stories and sharing mutual friends.

Stan Waterman had exquisite manners—a quality that stood out the night Mr. H. suggested a trip into town to the Hotel Internationale. This sounded intriguing, so we all piled into the boats and then the cars to go to town. When we arrived at the Hotel Internationale several things became quickly apparent. One was that the Hotel Internationale was a house of ill repute—aka a bordello. And the second was that Mr. H. was "a regular." "Sultry" was the word that came to mind—from the men lounging languidly on the veranda in front of the building to the even more languid young women who greeted Mr. H. warmly when we entered the dance hall on the ground floor. Mrs. H. had elected to remain at home, for reasons that were now obvious.

While Mr. H. was occupied with one of the women of the establishment, the music started. The next thing we knew, Stan Waterman was dancing what appeared to be a waltz with a rather flamboyant young lady. "My God, there's my father, dancing with a tart!" Gordy, Stan's charming twenty-something son, exclaimed. After the first dance, though, Stan brought her over to the table where Peter, Gordy, and I were sitting, watching Mr. H. with one eye and Stan with the other. Since Peter spoke fluent Spanish and Stan did not, he wanted Peter to explain to the young lady that he hated to occupy her time, since he was not going to accompany her upstairs. While Peter dutifully explained the situation, Stan bowed slightly—he could have been at a tea dance at Yale—and took his leave.

Nothing else on land quite lived up to the Hotel Internationale, and soon it was time to leave British Honduras behind. For decades to come, though, dive trips were part of our life—always with spoons at the ready. There was the month on

Grand Turk with Annabel, where Peter swam with dolphins. The trip off Baja with David, where we all swam with seals until we realized that we were in real danger: the bull seal thought that portly Peter was a rival for the affection of the ladies and began to show serious signs of aggression, forcing us out of the water pronto. There was the disappointing week on a sailboat in the Bahamas when I realized the problem with the captain and his wife was the ice tea they began drinking in late morning: it was Scotch.

There were water trips when it was too cold to dive, like our trip to the fabulous April Point in British Columbia where we caught and then ate the world's most transcendental salmon and cod, bald eagles swooping through the air and orcas breaching across the straits. Or my favorite boatel, the Last Resort Resort, a collection of houseboats and what are called float houses—little cabins attached to one of the archipelago of islands off the coast of British Columbia.

And the best dive trip of all, eighteen days on a sailboat on the Red Sea. Peter, David, and myself; Renzo, the Italian captain who became a beloved friend; Laurie, the nubile eighteen-year-old San Franciscan who was working her way around the world cooking; and Asher, the warm, wise Israeli divemaster. The diving was pure paradise, there was no shortage of food, and the camaraderie was intense. When Peter swam back to the boat on September thirteenth to find the five of us singing "Happy Birthday," with a blow-up birthday cake—complete with candles—floating by the dive ladder, he laughed and cried at the same time. And for once, he didn't need a spoon!

Mary Hemingway's Seviche

Caribbean sea urchins are best eaten while standing in the Caribbean. And we never made conch-anything at home. But being in the Caribbean always reminded Peter of Mary and Ernest and Cuba. This is Mary's recipe for the best raw fish ever.

¾ cup freshly squeezed lime juice
1 lb. raw fish (a firm white fish such as cod), scallops, or peeled shrimp
¼ cup coriander leaves, chopped
½ cup red onions, sliced, *optional*
¼ tsp. hot peppers, chopped, or a dash of Tabasco sauce, *optional*

Pour ¾ cup of freshly squeezed lime juice over the fish. (It is important that it be freshly squeezed; for some reason, this works better.) Add ¼ cup chopped coriander leaves. You may also add ½ cup sliced red onions and ¼ tsp. chopped hot peppers or a dash of Tabasco. Mix thoroughly.

Marinate for at least 1 hour in the refrigerator. The seviche can be kept for up to 24 hours but is best eaten within a few hours after mixing it.

The Very Best Herring

If you find yourself on a fishing boat in the Atlantic instead of a reef in the Caribbean, this recipe might appeal. It's very Peteresque!

3 herrings
3 lemons
3 cups ocean water

A herring is one of the most beautiful of fishes; its scales look as if they were chipped off a rainbow. Fresh from the sea, using sea water instead of salt, and a few drops of lemon (or no lemon at all), a herring is one of the most delicious things you could eat. Peter once told a Japanese chef that he had caught herring in the Atlantic and eaten it within 2 minutes of being caught. The chef looked at him with envy. Then he smiled and said he was going fishing.

Gravlax

This must be made with the finest salmon you can buy. Peter used to make this when Annabel lived in Seattle and could bring us incredible salmon from Pure Food Fish Market in the Pike Place Market. When faced with a daunting array of different kinds of salmon there, Peter asked the owner what he would serve his mother; Copper River King, he replied, so that is what we bought.

½ cup salt
¾ cup sugar
¼ cup pepper
¾ pound fresh dill, rinsed (use all of the dill, stems and all)
1½ lbs. salmon (bones removed, skin on)
Oil and lemon juice, to serve

Thoroughly mix salt, sugar, and pepper. Sprinkle ¼ cup of this mixture on the bottom of a pan approximately 12x6-inches and at least 2 inches deep.

Cover with ½-inch layer of dill, then add another ¼ cup of the salt/sugar/pepper mixture on top.

Lay fish on top of dill, skin side down. Using ½ cup of the remaining mixture, cover the fish completely. Cover with 1-inch thick layer of dill.

Cover pan with foil and place weights on top (Heavy cans are the simplest unless you have diving weights handy!). Place in refrigerator for at least 48 hours before eating.

Within an hour or two of being put in the fridge, your pan will be full of liquid. This is the liquid in which the fish will marinate. If it does not completely cover the fish, turn fish over during the marinating. The fish will keep up to 10 days in the fridge.

When you serve the gravlax, scrape off whatever layer of the mixture remains on the fish, but only from the part you are about to slice. Slice the fish off the skin in very thin slices, diagonally as you would cut smoked salmon. Return unsliced fish to the marinade immediately. Serve with a few drops of oil and a few drops of lemon juice.

A FINE RIPOSO

Peter loved taking a nap—a *riposo*, he would call it, in the Italian manner—or a *riposino*, if it were a catnap. And having carefully structured his life so that he never worked in an office, he was able to take naps with some regularity. The most memorable nap, however, was both unexpected and unconventional. It took place in Italy in a tiny *pensione* in the Appenine Mountains west of Modena.

Although balsamic vinegar was the stated attraction in our 1976 trip to Modena, the not-very-hidden agenda was food, scrumptious food. The region of Emilia-Romagna—home of

Bologna and all things Bolognese—offers a very good table indeed: the tenderest tiny pastas wrapped around delicate fillings, cotechinos, mortadella and a parade of other sausages, aromatic truffles. Peter and Michael and I tried to sample them all.

Michael summed up the results perfectly at the end of our first splendid dinner at the Fini Hotel. Unlike the average thirteen-year-old American, he had just polished off a *bollito misto* served from a great copper cart, formally rolled up to the table by two impressive waiters. When the huge dome was lifted, there were tender white chickens, beef, veal, a cotechino, even a calf's head, all simmered in broth. The waiters very formally served your choices with a green sauce made from an unforgettable blend of herbs, anchovies, oil, vinegar, as well as strangely wonderful *mostarda di cremona*—fruits pickled in some mysterious way with mustard. Although Peter and I had ordered delicious dishes, Michael clearly had won the dinner prize. Quite satisfied and quite full, Michael gazed about the elegant dining room. He surveyed his happy dinner companions (who were anticipating their very own *bolliti misti* the next night). With his usual acuity he observed, "Our mouths are having a *very* good time!"

Of all of the good times we had on that Modena trip, however, the most Peteresque was our lunch in the mountains. With directions from the inestimable Fini concierge, the three eaters set out early one morning to drive to a tiny village in the mountains. There, we were told, we would find a lunch worth the journey. In the back of my mind, of course, was the question of why we possibly would want lunch when we were going to dine at Fini that night, but I knew that protest would be futile and that an adventure was inevitable. So I set out with undue enthusiasm.

As we wound our way higher and higher through the hills, we spotted a sign announcing what was always an obligatory stop: Cheese Made on the Farm. In this case the sign was in Italian and the cheese was Parmigiano-Reggiano.

The delicate smell of "parm" directed us to a low, white-washed building near the entrance to the farm. Inside we found the farmer and a LOT of cheese. Hundreds and hundreds of huge wheels of Parmesan, shelf upon shelf of cheeses, carefully ranked by age. The farmer was testing them for readiness to ship to shops and restaurants in Bologna and Milan. To do this he pulled out the small "plug" he'd cut in the rind and inserted a special stainless-steel instrument with which he pulled out a tiny flake of cheese. Fascinated, we plied him with questions—that is, Peter plied him with questions in Italian and then translated for Michael and me. At that point in life, I had naively assumed that "Parm is Parm." I was woefully ignorant, needless to say. As we tasted tiny pieces of cheeses of different ages, our mouths learned the lessons the cheese had to teach. Older is nuttier, younger is lighter, and on and on.

One of the many things I learned while eating with Peter was that you never knew what was going to happen next. So, as the farmer showed us the steps in transforming milk into all of these nuanced versions of Parmesan, Peter was curious. "What happens to the whey?" he asked. "Ah," the farmer replied. "Come with me and you will see." He led us out of the cheese building and across a path to a nearby barn. The day was sunny and warm, and at first the only sound was birds singing in the mountain breeze. But then it started: the most unholy squealing and high-pitched shrieking I had ever heard in my life. Our mouths agape, Peter, Michael, and I looked at one another with a lot of puzzlement and a little apprehension. What in God's name was going on? As we entered the barn, we saw fifty shrieking pigs, snouts raised in the air. Clearly the pigs heard the farmer approaching and anticipated what was about to happen. The farmer smiled, held up a finger as if to say "now watch this," and flipped a switch. Piped in from the cheese building, the whey poured into troughs in the barn. Within an instant, to the sound of rushing liquid, it was all snouts down. Satisfied snuffling and slurping were the only sounds. The only sounds other than our laughter, that is. Both farmer and pigs seemed very pleased with themselves. When asked about the eventual fate of the happy pigs, the farmer said just one word: prosciutto.

Highly amused, we set out again to find the village and lunch. The road wound through pine forests, higher and higher into the mountains. By the time we reached the village, whose name I have long forgotten, it was almost noon. Everywhere we looked there were walkers, all Italian, taking their morning constitutionals in family groups. We had no trouble locating the hotel the Fini concierge had named, however, for all the walkers were strolling toward its door. Clearly this was *the* place to dine.

When I think back to that dining room, what I see is white. Unlike the sophisticated Fini dining room, carefully lit with warm muted light, this mountain dining room was filled with sunlight and freshly laundered linens. The walls were white, the tablecloths were white, and so were the carefully folded napkins that were the size of baby blankets.

We quickly realized that the hotel was *en pension*, and we settled back to be served whatever the former strollers were going to be served. And that was mushrooms. Marinated mushrooms for a first course. Mushroom soup. Pasta with mushrooms. Veal with mushrooms. There were many courses and they all were based on mushrooms—except dessert, fortunately. "It is the season," the waiter helpfully explained. The preponderance of mushrooms was unorthodox, but it didn't matter. One mushroom course was more exquisite than the next.

Also fabulous was the Lambrusco that accompanied it. When, after discussion with the waiter, Peter ordered a bottle of Lambrusco, I turned up my nose (always a foolish thing to do when Peter was ordering anything). In my experience—clearly limited at that point—Lambrusco was a sweet, very déclassé wine that no one in their right mind would drink. That was before I had Lambrusco where it comes from. That day in the mountain village I had my first taste of Lambrusco as it is supposed to taste: chilled, fruity, a delicious and refreshing accompaniment to the mushrooms. And light. So light in fact that Peter and I finished off a bottle of wine with the first few mushroom courses. The well-trained waiter then asked if we would like another bottle. "Heaven's no," I said to Peter, thinking of the winding mountain drive that would follow lunch. Finishing off one full bottle at lunchtime was already excessive, we certainly couldn't have another. But Peter did not look at it this way. He wanted more Lambrusco, but knew that some modicum of caution was needed. His response to the waiter was, I'm sure, a first: "Is there the possibility of a *riposo*, a nap?" he inquired. For a fleeting second, the waiter looked startled, but being the professional Italian waiter that he was, he inclined his head as if to bow and said that he would ask at the desk. Moments later he returned with an affirmative: Yes, there was a room where the three Americans could take a nap. "Wonderful," Peter responded, "then we will have another bottle of your wonderful Lambrusco." And so we did.

Fully sated and very happy after our meal was complete, we were escorted to a lovely hotel room with a bed for Peter and me and a bed for Michael. In minutes we were sound asleep—dreaming of mushrooms. An hour or so later, refreshed and still happy, we wound our way down the mountain and back to Modena where Fini and the *bollto misto* awaited us. How in the world we managed to eat that night is beyond me, but I know that our mouths had a very good time.

Divine Mushroom Soup (the Original)

In honor of the all-mushroom lunch. This is the recipe as Peter wrote it.

Make chicken broth using lots of chicken, some onion, and a little carrot. Strain broth, saving chicken meat (discard skin and bones). You should have about 1½–2 quarts of broth.

Chop 3 lbs. mushrooms (mixed varieties if possible, although this works with plain old white mushrooms as well) and boil for 2–3 minutes in strained chicken broth with 1⅔ cups cooking sherry and the chicken meat. Cool, uncovered, then refrigerate.

For every 3½ cups of liquid, add 1 cup heavy cream.* Blend very thoroughly.

*Peter used heavy cream—of course. I use buttermilk with a wee bit of cream poured in each bowl before serving.

Divine Mushroom Soup (an Adapted Version)

1 lb. chicken thighs (to make life easier you may want to use boneless skinless thighs)
6 cups good chicken broth
2 shallots, chopped
1 Tbsp. olive oil
1 Tbsp. butter
2 lbs. trimmed and sliced mushrooms (preferably an assortment of different kinds)
½ tsp. dried thyme
½ tsp. salt
Pinch of cayenne pepper
1 cup dry sherry or Marsala
2 Tbsp. parsley, chopped
1 cup heavy cream

In soup pot, simmer chicken thighs in the chicken broth for 25 minutes. Strain broth into large bowl and set aside. Remove and discard bones and skin from chicken if necessary. Shred chicken and reserve.

On medium heat, sauté chopped shallots with olive oil and butter in the soup pot for 2 minutes. Stir in the mushrooms. Add thyme, salt, and cayenne. Stir occasionally until mushrooms are almost cooked. Add sherry or Marsala and simmer until mushrooms are cooked and alcohol evaporates. Return strained broth and shredded chicken to soup pot and combine with cooked mushrooms. Simmer for 3 minutes to blend flavors. Then stir in chopped parsley and remove from heat. Cool to room temperature, then chill in the refrigerator (for several hours or overnight).

Before serving, stir in the heavy cream. The soup can be served cold or reheated to just below a simmer. Taste and adjust seasonings before serving.

Marinated Mushrooms

A somewhat lighter dish.

1 lb. mushrooms (any kind or a mixture will do)
1 cup good olive oil
2 Tbsp. lemon juice
1½ Tbsp. grated lemon peel
¼ cup thinly sliced lemons
1 egg yolk (or 2 tsp. Dijon mustard)
2 tsp. salt
¼ tsp. black pepper
½ cup chopped red onions

Rinse whole mushrooms in ice water, then cut off tips of stems and cut into thick slices. If large, cut in half. In a large bowl, place oil, lemon juice, lemon peel, thinly sliced lemons, and egg yolk. Stir well, then add mushrooms. Add salt, pepper, onions; stir.

Marinate in refrigerator for 8 hours, stirring gently every few hours. This is best eaten within 12 hours, before the mushrooms become too soft.

ADVENTURES IN THE RAW

It all started with a salad.

Peter's literary agent had come for dinner, the centerpiece of which was a large, complex, and delicious salad. Peter *loved* salad—he often called himself "the world's largest rabbit"—and the salad that evening involved watercress, endive, grapefruit, kumquats, strawberries, and peanut oil. I remember the ingredients from so long ago only because Peter later made a fantastic watercolor collage for my birthday, commemorating that salad.

In the course of conversation, Peter was playing with ideas for new books, and one of us said "what about a salad cookbook?" In today's "salad days" of eating, menus abound with composed salads that paint pictures on plates, chopped salads, three-colored salads, salads topped with thin slabs of Parmesan, salads with walnut or truffle oil. It's hard to recollect a time when—even in Manhattan—American menus and American homes thought a simple Caesar salad was daring, when iceberg was still a staple, and when tomatoes came in one color (red) and two sizes (regular and cherry). So Peter's salad creations, which would have been scrumptious at any time, were in those days so imaginative that they would inspire someone to suggest that he put them in a salad cookbook.

With a little investigation, however, we discovered there were other inspired salad makers and the world did not need more salad cookbooks. But by this time Peter's imagination was at work—an always productive and sometimes dangerous state of affairs. In this case, the result was an unexpected adventure that produced a non-cook cookbook and some very amusing moments.

He quickly titled the non-cook cookbook *Eat It Raw*. The children and I accused him of starting an authoritarian cookbook series, for he became so enamored with telling people how to eat that he began planning books like *Broil It*, to be followed by *Bake It*, *Braise It*, and on and on. It's probably just as well that series never came to pass. But once he had the idea for a raw food book, he approached it with his usual combination of intensity, intellectual and human curiosity, and precision.

Today, raw food is one of the many fads promising eternal health and (probably) sexual prowess. Even in the 1970s, people like Adelle Davis preached the health benefits of raw juices. But Peter started with the simple premise that raw food is delicious. Its health benefits were irrelevant in his pantheon of virtues. A perfect peach. An amazing tomato. A piece of fish fresh from the sea. Peter was all about the best of the best. If the virginal ingredient were perfect, what could taste better?

Peter's solution to all of life's challenges was a notebook. Soon there was a three-ring binder labeled "EAT IT RAW," in which he began collecting ideas, recipes, clippings, sources. First there were the dishes such as ceviche and gazpacho, raw dishes that Peter knew about from travels in South America and from living in Spain. There were recipes galore for these already, but Peter had his own secret sources. Mary Hemingway gave him the ceviche recipe that she and Ernest had created. And gazpacho—that required phone calls to Spain (this was years before we found ourselves at the center of that Great Gazpacho Contest between Antonio and Pilar). And there were other exotic recipes that Peter remembered from his travels, such as a Spanish soup of almonds, garlic, and forty peeled grapes!

Eat It Raw was not to be simply a compilation of other people's recipes, though. Everyone knows about steak tartare, but Peter set out to invent dozens of new sauces to have with it, all raw. He concocted new ways to serve raw fish, dozens of raw soups, drinks and sauces and salads. At first, it all went into the notebook.

In due time a book proposal was written, sample recipes created, and—in those easier publishing times—a contract was quickly signed. Now, it was time to write the book. For a cookbook, this means creating real recipes, recipes with lists of ingredients in precise amounts, recipes with instructions for every step. Peter was a fan of the old-fashioned French cookbooks that assume that you know how to do it all, where a recipe for *boeuf bourguignon* was a short paragraph long. But he knew he had to do this one differently.

Since fifteen-year-old Annabel was the dedicatee of this book, Peter planned the recipe creation for weekends, when she was not in school. The consummate planner, he organized the ideas to be turned into recipes so that everything using tomatoes was assigned to one weekend, everything using apples to another, and so on. Annabel was duly appointed as the scribe and installed at the kitchen counter, yellow legal pad and black Flair pen in hand, poised to write down the ingredients and instructions her father called out as he created dish after dish in portions for four. Consulting his big "idea" notebook, Peter concocted a dish, tried it out, and shared it with Annabel, the chief taster. Sometimes they smiled; sometimes they frowned; sometimes the creation was made again.

Meanwhile, the rest of the family was banished from the kitchen entirely. Periodically I peered in to see what was going on. Peter was most often standing at the blender (this was pre-Cuisinart), talking to Annabel, who was madly writing down quantities of the ingredient du jour: "Put three tomatoes in the blender. Count to four while you blend. Then add . . ." As my head peered around the door, Peter would shoo me away, as Annabel rolled her eyes and I chuckled at the scene.

Before each weekend, Peter would command, "Susan, please invite six people for dinner on Saturday night and four people for Sunday lunch"—or some similar combination. After all, someone had to consume all that food being churned out in the kitchen. We had game friends of all ages who were willing to come to meals with menus like seventeen kinds of tartare steak, fourteen soups, and twelve fruit desserts.

Eventually the book was published, and it was time to celebrate. First in order was a book party, and Annabel and I decided that we would provide the festivities, since even in those more halcyon days publishers were not inclined to spend much money on any book that was not a ready-made bestseller.

With a menu based entirely on *Eat It Raw*, of course, we made platters of crudités, gallons of raw mushroom soup, huge bowls of couscous "cooked" in lemon juice, ceviche, tartare steak with a dozen sauces, and an enormous fruit salad.

Everyone who was invited came. How often, after all, is one invited to A Raw Party, as Annabel's handmade invitations proclaimed? The guest list was as eclectic as the book and its author: There were the usual suspects in the publishing world, from the wild and wonderful agent who represented Peter's adult books to the editor-in-chief of the publishing company along with a bevy of twenty somethings from PR and marketing. There were family friends, from Mary Hemingway to Annabel's BFFs. And most important by far, there were The Purveyors, the quintessentially important people who had provided the ingredients for all those recipes.

These were the days before the proliferation of Greenmarkets in New York. If you lived on the Upper East Side of Manhattan as we did, you found the best ingredients in the small specialty grocers around the city, who you could telephone and who delivered your order to your door. It was an old-fashioned world of conversation and discussion, of running jokes and long time relationships. It was very human.

In at least one case, the relationship had begun in the late 1930s. When Elinor, Peter's mother, returned to New York after decades living in Europe, she could find only one store where she could buy the kinds of olive oil and other essential Italian staples that she was used to. It was Manganaro's on Ninth Avenue. Peter called the store once a week or so. The order was important: olive oil, prosciutto, fontina, pastina, and biscotti. But just as central to the call was catching up with the multiple generations of the Dell'Orto family, hearing the latest Ninth Avenue gossip from owner Sal, teasing whichever one of the Dell'Orto daughters may have answered the phone, analyzing just which of the recently arrived panettones was best. Placing an order took a while. Of course, the entire Dell'Orto family was invited to the party, and they all came.

Oscar came too, and brought his wife. Oscar owned Empire Fruit and Vegetable, a greengrocer on Madison Avenue. Just the name, "greengrocer," conjures up a simpler time past. Long before there were Korean markets and Whole Foods in New York, there were greengrocers, stores that specialized in vegetables and fruits, beautiful produce that the purveyors could discuss with you: "You don't want melons today, Mr. Buckley. You won't be happy with the cantaloupe, and the honeydew is too expensive." "Try the snap peas that just came in; they're perfect." "Ah, you want some Treviso? Well, let me try to find you some when I talk to my wholesaler." The stores may have been smaller and the prices higher than Whole Foods, but the service was on a whole different level.

And then there was Connie the Butcher (to distinguish him from other Connies in our lives). Connie was the butcher at Madison Star Market on Madison Avenue, another vestige of the past. These small markets were almost entirely based on telephone orders, and you could order everything from the finest sirloin to prosaic paper towels. Today in Manhattan there are almost no stores like this, but they still existed in the 1970s and Peter had grown up with them as long as he had lived in New York.

For the Raw Party, Connie had supplied what would now be an appalling amount of raw beef—pounds and pounds of it carefully ground no more than an hour before the event. Peter and Connie always discussed in some detail whatever meat was to be ordered. It was always a caring and jocular exchange, in which Peter was the acolyte at the feet of Connie, the master of meat. One of Peter's most salient characteristics was his great respect for anyone who knew what they were talking about. He asked questions and he listened—whether he was asking a head of state about a complex political situation or listening to a renowned bullfighter discuss the merits of bulls from one bull ranch versus another or asking a farmer why "black dirt" grew better onions than any other or inquiring from Connie just why he thought sirloin was the most flavorful cut for steak.

When the meat arrived on our doorstep, it was not in Styrofoam and plastic. It was wrapped in butcher paper, by the butcher. It was "Connie's tartar steak," not a package of supermarket anonymity. For the party, Annabel and I had placed the meat on a large silver platter in the middle of the table—a truly astonishing mound of cold, red, raw ground meat.

The party was just getting into full swing when the doorbell rang, and there was Connie, looking very shy. There is no question that he had never been to a book party before. He was dressed in a suit undoubtedly worn only to church or to funerals. Connie was a bachelor and, I imagine, called his mother in Ireland every Sunday.

I greeted Connie warmly, so happy that he really had come, that Peter's telephonic cajoling had worked. Then I led him over to the table, to show him that his meat had pride of place in the array of food. Connie may not have been an habitué of book parties, but he was a proud craftsman who took his work seriously.

I will never forget what happened next. Fluttering about the table was a flurry of publishing girls, one thinner and prettier and chirpier than the next. All were dressed in the requisite black of young, sophisticated, New York publishing "starters." And every skinny one of them had a plate piled high with Connie's tartar steak. "Have you EVER had anything more divine?" "Can you believe this?" they chattered to one another, consuming more raw beef in each mouthful than any of them had ever dreamt they'd have in a lifetime. The expression on Connie's face was beatific. Gleaming with pride and pleasure, confirmation that his life's work had value, he looked as though he had died and gone to heaven.

Pretty soon there was the buzz of a good party. The greengrocer was talking to the butcher. The Italian specialty shop owner was comparing notes on Italy with the widow of the Nobel Prize–winning writer. The kids were interrogating the publisher. And Peter, holding court from an armchair, was proclaiming on the incomparable flavor of *fraises de bois* freshly picked on a French hillside.

Annabel and I smiled at one another. It was the perfect celebration for a book whose main ingredients were good food and lots of imagination.

Couscous Salad

A recipe from our friend Francoise, which Peter adapted for Eat It Raw.

- 2 cups raw (uncooked) couscous
- 1½ cups lemon juice, *divided*
- 2 cups cherry tomatoes, halved
- 1½ cups chopped peppers
- 1½ cups whole mint leaves
- 1 cup raw, skinned almonds, broken into halves or large pieces*
- ½ cup olive oil
- ½ Tbsp. chopped hot peppers
- 2 tsp. salt

Spread couscous in a large flat dish. Pour 1¼ cups lemon juice over the couscous, wetting all of the grains; do not stir. After 15 minutes, rub the couscous between your fingertips. Repeat this rubbing in half an hour and then again in one hour.

Add tomatoes, peppers, and mint to couscous and chill for several hours. Before serving, add nuts, oil, hot peppers, salt, and remaining lemon juice.

*Since this recipe was adapted from *Eat It Raw*, the almonds were raw, but they're really much better if they're toasted!

Raw Mushroom Soup

Even using ordinary white mushrooms, this soup has a lovely delicate flavor. There is something about the effect of the food processor that "empowers" the mushrooms.

1½ lbs. mushrooms
4 cups whole milk
2 Tbsp. chopped white onions
2 Tbsp. good olive oil
1 Tbsp. lemon juice
2¼ tsp. salt
1 pinch cayenne pepper
1 cup cream

Rinse but do not dry mushrooms. Trim off hard tip from stems and cut into quarters. Blend/process together mushrooms, milk, onions, oil, lemon juice, salt, and cayenne pepper. Chill in the refrigerator. Stir in cream just before serving. Shake or stir well.

Best eaten within 12 hours.

TO MARKET, TO MARKET

Peter *loved* markets—all kinds of markets, all over the world. Partly it was the food, but he loved the humanity of markets just as much.

As a child growing up in Europe before the war, Peter took markets for granted. In Paris and Rome and London and Geneva and Vienna—the cities of his childhood—street markets were a fact of life. And then there were the grand "institutions" like Les Halles and Covent Garden. No A&P for little Peter.

The moment of truth came in 1960, however, in a vast and fabulous market in the Nigerian city of Onitsha. It was said to be the largest outdoor market in all of Africa—and all the sellers were women. Thousands of women selling food, cloth, pots and pans, medicines, snakes and birds, charms and potions—everything imaginable. As far as you could see in every direction, women were sitting on the ground on cloths, selling their goods, bargaining with buyers, and calling out to their neighbors—all in Igbo, a language the multilingual Peter understood not at all.

Peter, who had gone to Nigeria to write and photograph a children's book, was enchanted by the chaos and the energy and the raw humanity of this enormous market. And clearly the market women were enchanted with this tall white man in their midst—a rare occurrence in 1960—for at the end of their walk through the market, Peter's cicerone, a Nigerian lawyer named Luke, said, "Well, *you* certainly were a success today."

"What do you mean?" Peter responded, puzzled.

"As you walked through the market," Luke told him, "the women called out to one another, 'God must be great to make such a man!'"

Truly, it was the high point of what would be decades of market strolls. He *never* got over it.

While Peter was debuting in the markets of Onitsha, I was suffering through "mystery meat" and overcooked vegetables in a college dining hall in Vermont. It would be more than a decade before Peter introduced me to markets as an essential part of life, but when it happened, I was a prime candidate for falling in love with both the food and the humanity of markets. In Southwest Louisiana, where I have spent part of my life, good food is savored, debated, prized. Every morning of my childhood I heard my grandmother and Lucille Lyons, queen of the kitchen, discuss the day's dinner (always served at noon in the old-fashioned way). It was clear even to a child that this was an important discussion, that what we would eat was a matter of import and, for me, excitement, for Lou was a fantastic cook, famous throughout our little town. Would we be having red snapper or Spanish mackerel or some other tasty fresh fish my grandfather and uncle had caught in the Gulf the day before? Or would it be shrimp creole? Or Lou's famous fried chicken? Or corn bread and black-eyed peas that I mashed together just the way my adored grandfather did (and to the dismay of my far more proper grandmother)?

None of this truly delicious food came from farmers' markets though. Today, in our locavore world, there are wonderful farmers' markets even in Southwest Louisiana. But in the 1940s and 1950s, there were lots of farmers but no open-air markets in places like Louisiana. The farmers came to town with their vegetables, and they stopped at the homes of their regular customers. Later on, they came in pickup trucks, but in my early childhood there was Rufus, who came to town in a mule-drawn wagon. He had turnips and carrots and giant cushaws—a vegetable that Lou prepared in some mysterious way that resulted in mouth watering caramelized squash. In season he had tomatoes and beans and all kinds of greens (collard, mustard, and more). Compared with really good farm regions, though, the pickings were slim, for neither the soil nor the climate was conducive to growing many vegetables. The rest of our larder came from grocery stores. Knowing the food I take for granted in my lucky life today, I would be appalled at the state of the vegetables and meat and scrawny chickens that Lou had to work with. But somehow she turned it all into absolute heaven.

I also grew up knowing about farmers' pride, for Crowley—my Louisiana hometown—was the self-proclaimed "Rice Capital of the United States," surrounded by rice farms and full of rice mills and rice dryers. Whose rice was the best was a topic of great discussion for all of my childhood. And my first true love drove a pickup truck (a fancy one, but still a pickup truck) and his father was a rice farmer. So, I knew a lot about eating and a lot about farmers when I first began going to markets with Peter.

The first markets we explored together were in France, of course. In September of 1973 I stood on the Rue Mouffetard with the swirl of the morning market surrounding me and knew that my dreams of European adventure were coming true. Here I was with my new husband, standing in a market where Hemingway had surely shopped.

On the Rue Mouffetard, we walked along the cobblestone street, down one side of the market and up the other. I'd never seen anything like it. On my maiden voyage to Europe (literally and figuratively) ten years before, I was busily visiting museums and monuments, not markets where a gypsy sold bundles of dried lavender stored in panniers on the flanks of a tiny burro and women spread out their chicory so that the centers showed almost indecently. There were stands with a greater variety of cheeses than I had ever seen in my heretofore cheese-limited life. There were piles of haricots verts and the most gorgeous tomatoes you'd ever seen, lined up in rows in proper French precision. And the fruit—golden pears and mirabelles and apples—were out of a Cézanne still life.

Of course there were tourists, and travelers like ourselves (always an important family snobbery, the distinction between tourists and travelers), but most of the people at the Rue Mouffetard market were "real" people, shoppers who were buying all of this gorgeous and delicious food to eat. At home. For the meals they had every day. It was a revelation that has continued to give me pleasure and envy and inspiration for more than four decades.

This was the beginning of years of market adventures.

In London we got up in darkness to go to the fish market at Billingsgate and listened to the completely indecipherable Cockney conversations in the early morning café where the fishmongers went when the market closed.

We wandered through Covent Garden, where I was sure I would see Eliza Doolittle around every corner and where Peter found a man selling wonderful small signs. Spread out on a cloth on the sidewalk were the last poignant bits of someone's business, for Covent Garden, like Les Halles, was shortly to disappear:

Shop here with confidence and be sure of the best.
Please don't squeeze me until I am yours.
Fresh Salads Daily
Choice Eating

Peter bought them all, and they are still in my kitchen today.

And on trip after happy trip, there were the markets of France. The endless bounty in the markets of Lyons, lining the quais along the Rhône on one day and the Saône on another where you found everything you came to expect in every French market, but also more different kinds of *saucisson*—a Lyonnaise specialty—than you ever could have imagined.

And the bustling market in Arles that we came to know so well, where on Saturday and Wednesday mornings at one end you could find everything from the fish of the Mediterranean to the peaches and melons and strawberries and cherries of Provence. And at the other end, the temptations of Provençal tablecloths, pottery, and wooden bowls that forced us to calculate major engineering feats to figure out how to stuff more into our always-capacious luggage (we once left home with four bags, left France with five bags, and then went to Ireland, which we left with seven bags, but that's another story).

Then there were all the village and small-town markets: Fontvieille, St. Remy, Gordes, and all the little Alpine markets around Annecy that we stopped in every year. Each had its own character and its own specialties, like the tiny, melt-in-your-mouth goat cheeses in Gordes or the stand after stand of reblochon and Alpine sausages in Thônes.

The height of our market insanity came in the early 1980s on a month long sojourn in France. The exchange was ten francs to the dollar, and we had a station wagon for a month—both key factors in what transpired. It seems as though Peter planned the trip as a version of France's Greatest Hits, since we had not been there for several years (a gap that was not allowed to recur for the rest of Peter's life). We went to the Loire. We went to the Dordogne. We went to Provence. And we ended in the French Alps. In each of these regions there were delicacies and treasures that were then unattainable or far more expensive in the United States (remember that exchange rate). Why not buy birthday and Christmas presents for everyone? Why not buy these wonderful things we would so enjoy when we got home? Why not?

Who knows what we bought in the Loire, but in the Dordogne we went berserk. First we were in the land of geese. At every sign saying *Vente a la Ferme* (letting us know that there were delicacies to be bought at the farm), we turned down the road. We tasted. We bought: foie gras, pâté, terrines. It was so easy to put them in the back of the station wagon. And the prices were so amazing. And after all, they would last for years. Then, of course, we found ourselves a few kilometers away and we were in the land of ducks. Here were more terrines, more pâtés, more cans to stash in the back of the car.

This would have been bad enough, but we next headed to Provence. And then we got into real trouble. Planning to stop in Nyons, capital of olive oil, Peter had brought empty plastic jugs from New York. Remember that this was the early eighties and while you could buy perfectly acceptable olive oil in New York, the selection was far, far more meager than it is now, when every supermarket offers a selection of extra-virgin everything. So in Nyons we went to the olive market—everywhere, olives in every size, shape, and preparation—and we went to the olive oil purveyors in the shops that surrounded the market. We came away with about four gallons of olive oil—into the back of the car.

Then there was soap. Lots and lots of heavenly smelling soap; a Provençal specialty. And material from Soleidou, a selection that put Pierre Deux on Madison Avenue to shame. And dried lavender. And and and. Into the back of the car.

On and on it went. Each purchase seemed like *such* a good idea. Each purchase was a bargain. Each purchase fit so easily into the back of the station wagon. We only grasped the enormity of what we had done when we arrived finally in the Alpine city of Annecy, our last stop. There, the two waiters cum porters at the hotel began unpacking the car. Bag after bag, box after box, they carried it all into our small suite. Thank heavens there was a tiny front room in addition to our bedroom, for soon it was filled with the contents of the car. Peter began to laugh. Easy for him—he was going to Venice to work on a movie after this. I, on the other hand, was going back to my job in New York—with an entire station wagon's worth of products of France!

After a week or so in Annecy, where you'll be happy to know we bought very little—even we were chastened by the reality of what had come out of that station wagon!—it was time to leave. We packed. We stuffed. We bought another suitcase. Finally, we staggered to the airport. And when we got there, it was discovered that I was going home with . . . 450 pounds of baggage! It tells you everything about the difference between then and now that we had to pay only about fifty dollars in excess baggage charges and the airline desk clerks thought the whole thing was hilarious. It was another world indeed.

It took us a number of years, by the way, but we did eat every mouthful of all of that goose and duck! Still, I wonder at the excess of that trip. Thinking back on it now, I am appalled on one level, but on another level I realize what it says about Peter and France. I think Peter wanted to bring France home. France was where his heart lay. It was at the core of his being. Even though he lived all over Europe for the first thirteen years of his life, he spoke French before English, had a French governess, went to the Lycée, and later to the Sorbonne, had a host of French friends, and for decades went to France at least once a year. So when we were at home with olive oil from Nyons and pâtés from the Dordogne and soap from Provence, France seemed a little closer. And all the things we'd brought home had stories. Remember the funny woman with wild hair who sold that cheese in Gordes? Remember when we bought this pâté on the little farm near Sarlat? Remember the potter in St. Remy who made these plates? I used to call them "story things." Surrounding himself with France at home helped Peter miss it a little less.

Thank heavens, nothing ever matched the insanity of that month long, station-wagon-stuffing trip in the early 1980s. But, intrepidly, we continued to go to markets wherever we could: an olive market in Cádiz, a camel market in Cairo, the fish market in Venice—one more extraordinary than the next. But the market that played the largest role in our life together was right here at home.

By the early 1980s, the Union Square Greenmarket was the largest, busiest open-air market in the city's growing network of farmers' markets. For years, every Saturday morning that we were in New York, Peter and I spent hours at the Union Square market. A friend once described our progress through the market from one farmer friend to another: As Peter strode through the center of the market, he looked like the lord of the manor, surveying his crops. I, on the other hand, was the happy bailiff, managing the dog and the shopping cart, trading stories with the farmers, and paying for what Peter had grandly purchased.

Certainly our forays to Union Square were about food. It was deeply satisfying to smell the perfume of June strawberries wafting over the market. It was delicious fun to have Greenmarket dinners every Saturday night all spring, summer, and fall. It was astonishing to taste yet another new kind of pepper from Ted Blew's seemingly endless array. It was a blessing to have to decide which of Stanley's gazillions of lettuces to choose that week.

But mostly, what touched our hearts at the Greenmarket were the people, the farmers who became our lasting friends. First were the MacLarens. Peter returned from the market one day early on, when I had not been with him, saying that he'd had a first—someone addressed him in Latin at the market. He'd stopped at a new stand, Whippoorwill Farm, to check out the organic meat and heathery yarns being sold by Malcolm and Linda MacLaren. At some point Peter articulated his adamant opinion about something culinary. "*De gustibus non disputandem*," Malcolm—the Harvard graduate, former Hotchkiss teacher, now organic farmer—replied. Peter raised an eyebrow and duly noted that the MacLarens were a most civilized couple, as indeed they are. The Whippoorwill Farm stand soon became one of our main stops, where Peter would pull up a chair, sit next to Linda, inquire about what she was knitting that day, and then engage in their ongoing and always wry observations about customers, other farmers, life in general, and market gossip in particular.

Every Saturday the rounds were the same. Chew the proverbial fat with the MacLarens. Talk with Ted Blew about peppers and sunflowers. Talk to Stanley about farming "the black dirt" on his farm near Middletown, New York. Find out from Mr. Kent just which apples would make the best pie this week. Sit with Sal Quattrociocchi, where talking about poultry was only a small part of the banter. For several years, in fact, the most important topic of conversation was the beautiful Joyce Migliorelli who, with her brother Kenny, presided over the vast tables of vegetables at the Migliorelli stand just opposite the Quattro stand. When Sal and Joyce married, Peter was as pleased as if he had arranged it all by himself.

Year after year, Saturday after Saturday, those visits at the Greenmarket were at the heart of our week. In summer and fall especially, we bought a large proportion of our week's food at the market. The market's greatest gifts were the human relationships that accompanied that food—the friendships at the market and the knowledge that we were eating Sal's chicken with Joyce's spinach or Stanley's salad, Malcolm's leg of lamb with Kenny's corn and Ted's peppers and Mr. Kent's applesauce on the side.

For that's what markets are all about—food that real people have produced. And if you are very, very lucky, they're about food that friends have produced.

Transcendental Beans

A favorite summer salad, with green beans from the Union Square Greenmarket.

1 large or 2 small whole lemons, thinly sliced
½ red onion, thinly sliced
1 egg yolk or 2 tsp. Dijon mustard
6 Tbsp. olive oil
2 Tbsp. good red wine vinegar
A small amount (a few shakes) of a good hot sauce such as Tabasco
1 lb. cold cooked green beans

Mix all ingredients except green beans ahead and let sit (in the refrigerator if using egg yolks).

Pour dressing over beans and toss just before serving.

Picky Beef (aka Piquant Beef Flanken)

A Saturday night favorite when we could get MacLaren beef and Ted Blew's peppers at the Union Square Greenmarket. (Ted Blew, sadly deceased, became a specialist in all kinds of peppers, and the array at his farm stand at the market was breathtaking.)

1½–2 lbs. beef flanken*, cut in ½-inch strips

Marinade

- 8 scallions, chopped
- A fistful of fresh young ginger, thinly sliced
- 9 large garlic cloves, sliced
- 1 lemon peel, grated
- 5–6 Italian sweet peppers, roughly chopped (or, if you prefer, use a mixture of sweet peppers and hot peppers such as jalapenos)
- ¾ cup good olive oil, plus more for sautéing
- ½ cup good red wine vinegar

Combine all marinade ingredients. Marinate beef in the marinade overnight (or at least for several hours) in the refrigerator.

Preheat oven to 350°F.

Remove meat from refrigerator and bring to room temperature. Remove beef from the marinade, reserving the marinade. Dry the meat on paper towels (this is important for browning the meat later).

Saute beef quickly in a lightly oiled, very hot skillet; you may need to do this in small batches. (If you are using short ribs, you may need to cook a bit longer.) When all the meat has been browned, put it into the Dutch oven with about ¾ of the marinade (including the scallions, peppers, garlic, and ginger). Cover the pot and cook for about 20–30 minutes.

Cook rice in 2 cups mixture of the marinade and good chicken broth.

Rice

Peter was inordinately fond of plain white rice. But you can use Arborio rice to make an easy risotto.

- 1 cup Arborio rice
- ½ cup white wine
- 2 cups good chicken broth

Add white wine to rice and simmer until all the wine is absorbed. (You can do this step ahead of time.)

Before serving, add chicken stock to rice and simmer for about 6–10 minutes until all the stock is absorbed and the rice is tender. You barely need to stir. When rice is fully cooked, add the balance of the marinade and a couple tablespoons of unsalted butter. Heat briefly. You may wish to add some grated Parmesan to the rice.

*Flanken and short ribs are the same cut of beef. Flanken is cut into thin strips across the bones; short ribs are cut parallel to the bone. If you cannot find a butcher to cut the flanken, just use regular short ribs.

Spinach Salad

Farmers' market spinach is more work (it's usually pretty sandy), but the flavor is worth it.

½ lb. ordinary white mushrooms, trimmed and sliced
2 cups cherry tomatoes, halved
2 Tbsp. peanut oil
1 lb. spinach, thoroughly washed in cold water, picked to remove stems (In today's world of pre washed greens, you can also use packaged baby spinach or a mixture of spinach and arugula for a peppery flavor.)
Salt and pepper to taste

Marinade

- Juice of 1 lemon
- 2 Tbsp. olive oil
- ½ tsp. sesame oil
- 2 tsp. rice vinegar
- 2–3 dashes Tabasco
- ½ tsp. salt
- 1 tsp. Herbes de Provence

Combine all marinade ingredients.

Marinate mushrooms in marinade for 3–4 hours, stirring occasionally. Halfway through, stir in halved cherry tomatoes.

When ready to serve, mix mushroom mixture (with marinade) with peanut oil. Toss spinach with marinated mushrooms until wilted. Add salt and pepper to taste and toss again.

And here is a variation a friend created when making this recipe. Peter would have loved this, I think!

Heat the peanut oil in a large pan on medium heat. Add 1 clove chopped garlic. Cook until fragrant, then add spinach and toss until slightly wilted and just warm. Add salt and freshly ground pepper to taste. Off the heat, toss with the marinated mushrooms and serve immediately.

THE YEAR I WENT TO FRANCE WITH BOLSHOI PETE AND NORA

"You're taking your *dog* to France? Are you out of your mind?"

No one, not even fellow dog owners, could believe that we were taking Nora, our lively, three-year-old, seventy-pound Bernese mountain dog, on our annual excursion to Civilization. I had no qualms about being in France with Nora. After all, she was a very civilized creature herself. No, my nightmare had to do with the events that would take place between leaving our house in New York and arriving at the hotel in Paris—the process known as Getting There. Since Getting There entailed transporting not only me and Nora but also one very large husband, five very large suitcases, two very large carry-on bags, and one very large dog crate, matters were somewhat complicated.

Getting ready for Getting There began days before our departure. Nora's bag was packed (and sniffed) long in advance. It was a rather heavy bag in fact. In addition to a full wardrobe of leashes for all occasions, it contained eighty-eight carefully measured cups of dog food—four cups of Instant Dog per day for twenty-two days. Carrying any sort of food *to* France seemed like the rankest foolishness, but our trustworthy vet cautioned against the results of an abrupt change of diet. A canine case of Richelieu's Revenge was a sobering thought.

Peter had carefully labeled Nora's crate with *Nora, Nom du Chien* on all sides. ("Obviously Air France will want to call her by name," he pointed out, miffed at my amusement.) Normally, Nora's crate sat open in our bedroom and she treated it as her house, a place to retreat to when the human action got too active. Now she was very puzzled to find it, with a door, sitting amidst an Alpine tower of suitcases.

Finally we had said goodbye to all of our friends in Central Park: Poochie and Hawthorne and Merlin, Joker and Schmata, Dylan and Zoe, Nicholas and Alexander (Russian wolfhound brothers, of course), Roscoe and Exxon (because he was found covered in oil), Joia and her two Samoyed sons.

Their owners shook their heads in amazement at our folly but wished us Godspeed and good eating.

Like a good traveler, Nora had her papers in order. A rabies certificate and a guarantee of good health were all that she needed. (This was 1992. Who knows what TSA would require today.)

At last it was time to leave. At four o'clock on a hot May afternoon, Ilya arrived in his battered station wagon to take us to the airport. It was Ilya, a Russian driver—minute of body but large of soul—who had long ago dubbed Peter "Bolshoi Pete," Big Pete. Even Ilya, usually undaunted by the Traveling Buckleys, looked somewhat appalled by the prospect of transferring the enormous quantity of bodies and bags from the sidewalk to the car. Bolshoi Pete barked out instructions. Nora just barked. I felt faint. "Would Scotch be appropriate at this hour?" I wondered, remembering our hard-drinking hostess in British Honduras. Valium perhaps? But there was no time for such silliness, for I soon found myself stuffed into the back seat of the car. Nora, wedged in next to me, promptly decided that my lap was the only safe place to sit, a decision that she would make frequently over the next weeks.

Leaving a trail of open mouthed doormen and skycaps behind us, we managed to affect the transfer from home to Air France with a maximum of barks (Bolshoi Pete's). At every turn I counted heads (three), bags (seven), and crate (one) to be sure we had lost nothing in the shuffle.

At last, Peter had installed himself in the waiting room, the checkable bags were checked, and it was time to deal with Nora. "*Le chien est . . . grand, très grand . . . et très actif,*" the sleek Air France agent observed with Gallic skepticism as

Nora bounced up and down in front of the counter, clearly intrigued with all of these new humans to nuzzle. I recalled that the last dog I'd seen on a flight to France was a very small, very French dog neatly tucked into an elegant Céline carrying case. Not our Nora!

With typical French efficiency, however, the plans were laid out. "It is hot," Air France said. "The dog must not sit outside on the airfield in her crate." (No, No, NO, I agreed, with visions of our beloved dog in the path of the afternoon's parade of 747s.) "Bring her back twenty minutes before departure," I was directed.

So Nora and I walked and Nora sniffed—and walked and sniffed some more. Soon The Great Water Problem presented itself. For days before our departure Peter and I had debated this question endlessly. The permutations were myriad: How much water do you give your dog—and when—before you incarcerate the poor animal for many hours in the hold of an airplane? Either too much or too little can have dire results. But now it was hot and I threw caution to the winds as Nora panted beside me. Clearly, too much water would be better than too little. Nora agreed.

Although Nora continually dragged me to the door past which Bolshoi Pete had disappeared, I managed at last to direct her back to her crate at the check-in counter. Very cautiously, very quizzically she entered her familiar haven only to emerge immediately. Clearly, something is *very* peculiar, she seemed to be saying. "I think I'll stay with you on the outside, thank you very much."

Good dog that she was, eventually with some reluctance she allowed herself to be enclosed and gently carted away by the Air France baggage man. Nora looked resigned. I look distressed. "*Tout va bien, madame. Restez-vous tranquille*," the Air France agent reassured me. Having immense faith in the innate efficiency and true kindness of most French people, I accepted her advice.

And she was right. All did go well—eventually.

Hours of transatlantic fretting passed: Was Nora still alive and if so was she thirsty? Could she conceivably escape from her crate? Would my human traveling companion ever stop stealing my pillows?

At last we arrived at de Gaulle, uninspiring entryway to Civilization. By this time we felt most *un*civilized as we dragged our sleepy, rumpled selves off the plane. I could see immediately that Air France had taken all necessary precautions. One wonders if there is a giant computer in the sky that transfers crucial information from one airline to another? Had our usual carrier, Swissair, actually told Air France ahead of time to have a small army of attendants to take care of the Traveling Buckleys? Having grown up in Europe in the days when there were few travelers and many porters, Peter expected nothing less and somehow in life always managed to get it. Sure enough, there were not one but two Air France helpers awaiting us. Because he had a bad knee then, Peter needed a wheelchair to take him the long distance from the plane to the car rental spot. And with our Alpine (Himalayan perhaps?) tower of luggage, we needed even more help. Soon Bolshoi Pete was in a wheelchair pushed by a willing but non-Bolshoi Air France man. The second Air France man and I managed the two overflowing luggage carts.

Now we had to find sweet Nora. Our Air France guardians assured us that she would arrive in her crate on a nearby elevator. We waited impatiently until the elevator door opened and seventy pounds of wriggling Bernese mountain dog flung herself from Peter to me in an ecstatic frenzy of reunion. Considerably less ecstatic was yet another Air France attendant, attached to the end of Nora's leash.

The Great Water Problem surfaced once more. Never again (we did this three times over the years) would I forget to have water waiting for the Emergence Ceremony. But this time I had. "*Mais pas de problem*" (an appallingly universal phrase), M. Air France announced, rushing to a nearby coffee bar. "She will drink Evian." Nora thanked him wetly.

Once again we counted, our troop now enlarged: Peter, me, and Nora; three Air France attendants; five large bags, two carry-ons, and one large dog crate. The caravan moved on, with Peter, of course, in booming command. We were off to claim the Renault Espace that we had reserved long in advance, sure that this spacious and wonderful vehicle would be just the thing for our entourage. The car was produced, all the luggage was stowed, and we tried to get in. A disaster!

Bolshoi Pete was indeed quite grand, as Ilya had observed. The problem, however, was not his rather capacious avoirdupois, but his rather enormous height. The Espace was then constructed in such a way that a six-foot-four-inch driver could not fit his legs into the space next to the gear-shift console. There was *no* way Peter could drive this car. Another must be found and fast.

Unfailingly polite and helpful, our Air France "staff" began to suggest solutions. But the day was saved by Mamoun, the North African man who supervised the rental car lot. Surrounded by luggage, the five adults and one dog were in great and audible consternation in the middle of a very large parking lot outside of a very large de Gaulle terminal. Within minutes Mamoun began producing cars for Peter to "try on" as if in a Savile Row fitting room. There were cars with high roofs that would fit the driver but not the luggage and long cars that would fit the luggage but not the driver. At one point Nora and I went inside to plead with the rental car people and when I emerged Peter was at the wheel of what could only be described as an enormous bread truck. Somewhat plaintively (a quality never before known in my spouse), he inquired whether I thought that this would do. It would not, I said firmly.

Finally a makeshift solution was found. One particular station wagon met all the requirements—but it was already rented. If, however, we could manage to get into Paris, we could have such a car that afternoon. So, with a zeal that could only have come from the prospect of getting rid of us,

Mamoun and the Air France men began to stuff all of us and all of our belongings into a smaller car. It was inconceivable, however, that Peter could drive this car; it was much too cramped. So I would have to drive it, but I had not driven a standard shift car—the only kind available—since I terrorized my high school driver's ed teacher more than thirty years earlier. Nonetheless, the only way to get to Paris and sleep was for me to drive the car and for Peter to hold Nora in his lap (since every other available centimeter in the car was crammed with dog crate and bags). It was an unforgettable drive.

"Clutch, shift, clutch, shift," Peter barked as I desperately tried to remember those long-ago lessons. After trying to jump out of the window, Nora just barked. I just clutched—the steering wheel that is. Finally and jerkily we waved farewell to our stalwart helpers and set out into the rush hour traffic of Paris at noon. If you have never been in the middle of thousands of French drivers trying to get to their noonday meal, you have *no* idea what rush hour really means. When at one point I ran a red light in the middle of a huge intersection, the gendarme who stopped the car took one look at my face, at the human, canine, and baggage contents of the car, shook his head, and waved us on.

Somehow, miraculously, we managed to reach the hotel and explode out of the car. We had, at last, Gotten There.

The next stage, Being There, was far easier than Getting There, of course. I'd always known that the French are almost as besotted with their dogs as the British, but being at the other end of a leash in France was a whole new adventure. Unlike hotels and restaurants in the United States, the majority of whom react in horror (and with legal threats) when they see a dog, the red Michelin guide indicates the few establishments that do *not* allow dogs. The assumption always is that dogs are welcome. Of course, most French dogs that you see tucked quietly under tables are not quite the size our Nora was, but nonetheless.

Nora had a lovely time on that and her two subsequent trips to Civilization. Her first Parisian meals set the tone: we fed her a long-overdue breakfast on the tiny balcony of our hotel room, where she could look out over the gray roofs of Paris in what looked like something out of a Marcel Carné movie. Later, feeling that all three of us surely deserved a treat after our exhausting arrival, we went for dinner to a slightly fancy restaurant near the Arc de Triomphe. As soon as we were seated a waiter approached the table with a small bowl of water for *le chien*, but when he saw her size he immediately turned around and returned, twinkle in his eye, with a champagne bucket, which he placed in front of the *chien* instead. And with our dinner came a separate plate. Clearly it was expected that we would put it on the floor to share some of our dinner with said *chien.* Of course we did just that. Nora proceeded to behave perfectly, though she preferred sitting up next to the table to survey the passing scene rather than hiding under the tablecloth. This was her first trip to Paris, after all.

It was the start of three trips worth of adventures: the time she got tired of sitting outside the open window of the restaurant and jumped right into the dining room to sit next to our table; the time she met her first cow in an Alpine standoff (the cow won); her first mistral in Provence, when the wind blew for three days without stopping and all the animals, including

Nora, paced without stopping; the year she got sand fleas when we went to Île de Ré, off the coast of Brittany, and Peter said—in all seriousness—"I don't think Nora is having as good a time this year as she usually does."

Most of the time, though, eating with Peter and Nora turned out to be even more fun than eating with Peter.

Nora's Favorite Dog Biscuits

Adapted from Paula Deen, this is the kind of treat Nora gobbled up.

¾ cup nonfat or 1% milk
1 egg
1 cup natural, smooth peanut butter (unsalted)
2⅓ cups whole wheat flour
1 Tbsp. baking powder

Preheat oven to 325°F.

In a large bowl, mix together the milk, egg, and peanut butter.

Add in the flour and baking powder. (The mixture will be stiff, so you may need to use your hands to work in the flour fully.)

On a floured surface, roll out the dough to about a ¼-inch thickness. Cut into small pieces or use a biscuit cutter, depending on the shape and size you want.

Bake on a parchment-lined pan for about 20 minutes. Turn the biscuits over and bake for 15 minutes more.

Allow biscuits to cool completely before storing in an airtight (and dog proof!) container. The biscuits freeze well, for up to 3 months.

DINING AT TABLE 2

If I could choose one moment, one time and place, in all my adventures in eating with Peter—in *being* with Peter—it would be something like this:

We have just arrived in France for our annual stay. It's either May or September, a day warm enough for us to sit outside on the terrace at our hotel, Pavillon de L'Ermitage, under the chestnut trees, looking out at Lake Annecy—the Alps at one end of the lake and the city of Annecy at the other.

We're a little jet-lagged after our overnight flight and the hour drive from Geneva to Annecy, but mostly we are deeply contented, knowing we are in our favorite place in the world and about to have yet another adventure over the next three or four weeks. It's all ahead of us, with none of the glitches—yet—that inevitably occur in real life. It was a scene that happened once or twice a year for more than a decade, beginning in 1983.

We had arrived to the delighted welcome of Madame Tucci, as we called her—Georgette Tuccinardi, wife of Maurice Tuccinardi, the chef and proprietor of L'Ermitage. As always in the traditional arrangement of traditional establishments like L'Ermitage, Madame Tucci was in charge of "the front of the house"—i.e., the dining room itself and the hotel (if there was one, as in this case), and the chef was in charge of the kitchen, which was of course the heart, the raison d'être, of the whole enterprise.

We've been installed in our rooms—always the same small suite with two rooms, one overlooking the lake. We've sniffed the bouquets of roses from the garden always placed there and then descended to the terrace. (I can still see Peter with a vase of roses in hand, *les roses portables*, Madame Tucci always called them.) The *tisanes de tilleul* (linden) were instantly provided as a pick-me-up to sustain us until lunch. And if it were one of the years when we brought Nora, a bowl of water and a little snack would have been produced for her as she lay contentedly at our feet, clearly relieved to be off the airplane and out of her crate.

Peter would have his ubiquitous packs of five-by-seven index cards with a card for each day of our stay divided into columns for DO and CALL. (This was how Peter organized his life, whether he was in the Sahara or New York or on an Alpine lake.) Peter with his black Flair pen in hand, me with the maps, we would begin to plot our course. For years, our pattern was the same: five or six days in Annecy; then off for some adventure, often in Provence; then back for another few days in Annecy.

As we luxuriated in the thought of three or four weeks of heaven, the same action was always going on around us. Sitting on the terrace we could hear noise from the kitchen: Tucci shouting out orders to his sous-chef, whisks whisking, the banging of pots and pans. Drifting out onto the terrace, the perfume of butter browning, stocks bubbling, mushrooms sautéing. Then Tucci's voice speaking tenderly to his mother, for sitting in a wheelchair just off the kitchen, peeling potatoes (always potatoes for his transcendental gratin) was Tucci's ancient mother. All dressed in black with a white apron, a bowl of potatoes in front of her, she was unable to stay away from the action of the restaurant. So every morning her daughter brought her to L'Ermitage. The mother spoke not a word of English, of course, but very little French either, though she'd come to France from northern Italy half a century earlier. She adored Peter, who always spoke to her in Italian and kissed her hand in a courtly fashion.

At some point not long after we sat down, Tucci—a thin, wiry man with bright twinkly eyes—would run out from the kitchen. Everything was always done at a run just before lunch or dinner. Vigorously shaking our hands, he welcomed us with his intense, rapid-fire greeting. How long will you be here now, and for how many days when you come back, he would ask. All of this in French, of course, as he spoke no English either. Once we gave him our schedule, he would nod and rush back into the kitchen, wheels clearly turning as he plotted out what he would cook for us on this year's visit.

Meanwhile, through the big windows open into the dining room we could see Madame Tucci and the two Thierrys (for years both waiters were called Thierry—we dubbed them Thierry Un, the older taller one, and Thierry Deux, smaller and younger). Under Madame Tucci's watch, they were spreading thick, glowing white linen tablecloths on the twenty or so tables in the dining room. Sometimes the Thierrys were ironing the cloths directly on the table so that each was perfect, smooth and soft and immaculate. Silver and crystal next, with a small bouquet of roses at each table. We could see our table, Table 2, the best table in the dining room, in the center of the wall of windows overlooking the rose garden and the lake.

Just thinking of Table 2 makes me sigh happily but with great longing. I found the beginning of a diary from one spring trip sometime in the 1980s. May 1, it is dated. "First meal in France in six months—sigh!" And then I listed what we were served for lunch that day: white asparagus with two sauces; one was whipped crème fraîche with chopped herbs; the other was a vinaigrette of oil, vinegar, and mustard. "Asparagus impossibly sweet and divine," I wrote. Then we had a "mouth watering" gratin, an unusual ratatouille-type vegetable mixture, and tiny haricots verts. "Peter wishes special mention to be made of the wine and cheese that followed," I wrote. The cheese was a Coulommiers, a soft brie-like cheese that Madame Tucci pronounced "*extra*"—a high compliment in her book. The wine was a "divine Moulin au Vent."

A few days later I noted a dinner of *ris de veau* (sweetbreads) served on tart apples with a cream sauce, plus a dish of wild mushrooms that merited a happy sigh in the diary. A later dinner began with *chou vert*—a young green cabbage available only two weeks a year, along with a tiny bird, a *pintade*, cooked in Jerez vinegar.

When we began this enduring relationship in 1983, we were simply welcomed with the warmth but formality of the always "correct" French. But like everyone in France, the Tuccinardis were fascinated by Peter's impeccable French and could not believe he was not a native. And soon Peter's irrepressible personality and his deep knowledge and intense curiosity about all things French completely fascinated them. Plus, he was a writer and for the French—at least the traditional French—no matter what their own profession, a writer is a person of respect. They loved me dearly and often marveled at my ability to deal with my oversized, outsized spouse, but it was Peter who was at the heart of this relationship.

It was unheard of for Chef (as the entire *équipe*—team—called him, like a first name) to come out of the kitchen to talk to *les clients*. But since we were staying in the tiny hotel attached to the restaurant and were hanging around the terrace all the time, Peter soon began to catch Chef in a quiet moment. He peppered him with questions. Peter wanted to know where those mushrooms came from. How did Tucci cook the huge Breton artichokes to such perfection? What was the best fish in the lake? Do snails really have to fast for a day before you cook them? And on and on.

After a few years, Tucci began to plan our stays around the food he wanted to cook for us. Our visits evolved into a marathon of *les surprises*. It really began when either Peter or I one day mused aloud that we would love to have soup as a first course for dinner. Ah, Tucci's eyes twinkled. "*Bien sur.*" That night Thierry Un arrived at Table 2 with a lovely white tureen and ladled out a superb soup—some sort of velouté of carrots, as I recall. We loved it, so Peter indicated to Thierry that he would like another serving. "*Attends, M. Buckley,*" "Wait," Thierry said. He then left for the kitchen and returned with another tureen with another soup. Nothing would do, of course, but that we try this one. It was another vegetable soup, equally delicious. Now the game was afoot, for sure enough, when we finished soup number two, a third tureen arrived! It was a fish soup more delicious than any soup either of us had ever tasted. Thierry was highly amused. Peter and I were happily full. But . . . we had commanded (we used to translate all sorts of things into franglais, so *commander le repas* became "commanding the meal") a main course of some nature and a dessert as well. It was all too much, as there was no way we could not eat everything we had ordered. It was like having a proverbial Jewish mother in the kitchen. "What's the matter? You don't like it?" Returning dishes uneaten would have been unthinkable.

The next day when Peter pointed out to Tucci with some amusement that three soups to begin the meal seemed a bit excessive, Tucci told us about his days doing a *stage* (apprenticeship) with Mère Brazier in Lyons. The robust Mère Brazier, the first woman to win three Michelin stars, was a good friend of the famous (and even more robust) Fernand Point. One day when Monsieur Point came to have lunch with Madame Brazier, the young Tucci was asked to produce three rich soups for them, which they followed with a bowl of strawberries and a quart of crème fraîche. Our soup marathon was nothing in comparison, he noted. What we soon realized was that we'd better not command *anything* ahead of time—at least not for lunch—as *les surprises* would be quite enough.

Sunday lunch was probably my favorite meal of all. Sitting at Table 2, I could see the shining lake on the other side of the huge windows, and the whole quietly buzzing dining room on the other. Like Sunday lunch in my childhood, there was always something special about it, everyone dressed up from church or just out for the occasion. There never seemed to be any tourists at L'Ermitage. It was all locals and a few "travelers" like us, regulars who came every year.

I think *contented* is the word I'd use to describe the dining room at L'Ermitage. Full, as there might have been about fifty happy diners. The room buzzed with gentle conversation, never noise or clatter. Madame Tucci was in charge, graciously making sure that all had what they wanted when they wanted it. Peter used to call her Eagle Eyes, for she could see absolutely everything happening in the dining room at the same instant. She took every order herself, always writing it down in pencil on small pads provided by an obscure coffee company. When we paid our bill at the end of our several-week stay, Madame Tucci always included all of the little papers, pinned together with a straight pin. I still have hundreds of them, reminders of years of lunches and dinners, years of dishes I'll never have again, dishes from the traditional repertoire of perfect French cuisine and dishes Tucci had created himself. In our day, L'Ermitage had one Michelin star. It had had two, but at some point Tucci consciously decided he no longer wanted to maintain that level of haute cuisine. He was happier with one star—and so were we. Peter and I always concurred that one-star restaurants were the best of all, memorable food without the formality—and sometimes preciousness—that came with two or three stars.

The two Thierrys were consummate waiters, professionals in every move, from boning your fish to knowing just the moment to ask if you wanted anything more from the dishes on the serving table. And I finally learned to say *J'ai fini*—"I have finished"—rather than *Je suis fini*, which means "I am dead!" Unlike speedy restaurants of today, places like L'Ermitage followed the tradition of serving each plate from a serving table set beside your table. The whole fish was brought and boned in front of you. Vegetables each arrived in their own gleaming covered silver dish, to be served onto your plate, always with a little left for a second serving.

One of the most memorable of all our L'Ermitage stays was my fiftieth birthday celebration. When Peter had asked what I wanted to do for my semicentennial, I knew right away. I wanted to have a "house party" in Annecy. So he arranged it all. Friends came from Paris and Bologna. Annabel arrived from her home in Seattle as a surprise. And close friends from Annecy were invited.

Of course, given Peter and Tucci, the excess began the day before my birthday. Recently I found a journal that I'd kept for those days, recording what we ate. It is hard to imagine now: to celebrate the arrival of Annabel (whom the Tuccis adored), Chef exceeded even his usual standards. There were not one but four *surprises* for lunch. We consumed (over several hours, mind you) the lightest imaginable mille-feuille with foie gras and its gelée between the "leaves" (surprise number one); tiny pieces of *pied de porc* (calf's foot) on crisp little potato pancakes (surprise number two); pasta in a cream sauce (surprise number three); and a perfect apple tart (surprise number four, which we had the wisdom to ask the Thierrys to save until dinner).

For dinner that night, we did show some wisdom and so did Tucci, as there were no surprises: only soup, a little smoked salmon, and a salad of frisée. And the apple tart, of course.

The next day was my semicentennial birthday. Our friend Renzo arrived from Bologna, clearly a cause for celebration, though the actual birthday dinner would not take place until the following day. I noted only one surprise that day. Tucci was saving them up for the official birthday dinner. For lunch we had leeks with vinaigrette, swiss chard with cream sauce, a selection of cheese, and the surprise: crème brûlée with braised cherries on top, a perfect combination of sweet and tart. And after that modest lunch, we were able to eat for dinner: artichoke hearts from the huge Breton artichokes that were one of Tucci's specialties, steak au poivre with béarnaise sauce, and what I recorded as "*les désserts*," which means the plates of petits fours and cookies that Tucci made every day (in his spare time).

The next day as more friends arrived, Renzo, Annabel, Peter, and I knew we were facing the official Birthday Dinner. So we got our exercise by walking through the Saturday antique market on the streets of the old town in Annecy and wisely eating only green beans and salad for a Spartan lunch.

Finally it was time. It was a beautiful May night, warm breezes coming off the lake, a deep blue sky as night fell. The lights of Annecy twinkled like a Christmas tree at one end of the lake and the Alps glowed in the sunset at the other. French, English, and Italian flowed around the table like the champagne the Thierrys kept pouring. "Many many laughs and much friendship," I recorded later that night.

Dinner was perfection. I'd asked for some of my favorites: We began with thin slices of Tucci's own version of gravlax with two sauces: one mustard sauce and one crème fraîche sauce. Then his signature dish, which was *soufflé de brochet*, quenelles made with one of the fish unique to the lake.

Finally, I'd asked for a fruit tart, my favorite of many favorite Tucci desserts. I was surprised when the first dessert Thierry Un brought out was a coffee parfait. It was excellent, but not my fruit tart. Hmmm. When we finished, I asked if anyone wanted a second serving. Instantly, Thierry looked alarmed. With the subtlest shake of his head he indicated that this would not be a good idea. He turned and went back to the kitchen. Out he came with the promised fruit tart, an enormous tart made with caramelized rhubarb and whole strawberries. Ah, we all sighed, and managed to find room for a second dessert. But it was not over yet. Finally, out came the pièce de résistance, the most beautiful birthday cake I've ever seen, covered with spun sugar like caramel lace (in French it is *les cheveux des anges*—the hair of angels). It was totally, completely, divinely delicious. When I blew out the candles, I could see Tucci peeking out of the kitchen at the end of the garden, smiling and immensely pleased with himself. It was the best birthday I ever had.

Amazingly, we actually did more than eat in Annecy. For one thing, we made friends over the years, and every precious day we planned visits with one or another of them. Perhaps we drove along the lake to the picture-postcard village of Talloires to visit Assunta and Jacques Chatelain at their antique shop filled with exquisite Alpine treasures, to hear about their latest adventure in the Sahara, where Jacques—and sometimes Assunta—took off every winter in his Land Rover outfitted with special water tanks and sleeping platforms.

Or we drove way up into the mountains to see Gaston Perillat-Colombe and his family, who lived at the top of an Alpine pass. They had been making cheese—reblochon, to be exact—every day, 365 days a year for as long as anyone could remember. If you asked Gaston how long his family had been making cheese, he would shrug his shoulders and throw up his hands in a caricaturish Gallic gesture. "Forever" was the answer.

If we were lucky and the time of year was right (from when the snows melted in the spring to the early fall before they came again), the cows were way up in the Alpage, the high Alpine pasture where they'd been taken to feast on the spring and summer grass. Best of all were the times we arrived on the very day the cows were being taken up or brought down. There are few sounds in the world that will transport me to bliss as quickly as the sound of fifty cowbells clinging and ringing through the air as the herd makes its way up the road to or from its summer home high above the already-high village where they spend the winter.

We'd met Gaston and his wife Giselle and their children on one of our earliest trips to Annecy. Peter being Peter decided we should drive as high up into the Alps as we could go in the car, on a road. Knowing the Haute-Savoie, he was pretty sure we'd find some cheesemakers at the end of the road. And sure enough, that first day, the car climbed and climbed around breathtakingly terrifying hairpin turns, rock escarpments on one side, meadows filled with cows sloping down vertiginously on the other (hence sparking the old jokes about Alpine cows whose legs were shorter on one side than on the other). And after about an hour, we could see a chalet and barns high above. The chalet looked like something out of *Heidi* or *The Sound of Music*, with its steep pitched roof and all of the cow-bells hanging from the roof around the front of the house. When we reached the top, we were greeted first by three or four suspicious herding dogs and then by the puzzled but warm smiles of Gaston and Giselle. Shortly, though, as could happen with Peter all over the world, we soon found ourselves sitting inside at the family table. Gaston cut down a smoked ham hanging from the ceiling and began to slice pieces off to go with the absolutely perfect wheel of reblochon cheese made yesterday from the milk of the cows we could see in the Alpine meadows surrounding the chalet. First clustered around the fringes and then summoned to lunch with us were the four children, fascinated by these two Americans who had wandered into their midst, one of whom spoke perfect French while the other spoke some strange variation of French words unlike any accent they had heard before (that would be me).

Today, the children are adults, still making cheese, still bringing the cows up to the Alpage. But at the chalet there is a restaurant, run by the daughter, Sylvie, for the tourists who more and more mount the road to the picturesque chalet. I've been up to see the family and to reminisce about Peter and *les annees passé*, but it's not the same.

I often think of those days high in the Alps, though. In a corner of my living room is an enormous, real cowbell I once had made for Peter's Christmas present. It was one of my more inspired gifts in years of trying to figure out what in the world to give this man who already had so many treasures. Gaston and Giselle had had special bells made for the lead cows to wear going to and from the Alpage. The bells were cast with the names of each child. So one year I had a special bell made. On the huge leather strap are our initials P & S B, in brass nailheads. And on the big specially cast bronze bell it reads "1992—Peter and Susan—La France Toujours."

For years, before the advent of laptops and cell phones, part of being abroad was reading the *International Herald*

Tribune. So after breakfast and after the daily consultation between Peter and Chef, we drove around the lake to town, to get the *Trib*. Obligatory while in town was stopping for a chat at the Fromagerie du Lac where Raymond Michel held forth. "*Enfin* (at last)," he would salute us, as he picked out a reblochon—his specialty—for our lunch. Picking it out always involved a whole riff of provocative conversation with Peter as Raymond was in perpetual motion, picking up several cheeses, tapping them gently with his fingers, sniffing them, then checking out another. The shop would be crowded with people also getting their cheese for lunch. It was a completely local audience—housewives doing their morning marketing, always well-dressed, perhaps a pleated skirt and a cardigan, with a silk scarf tied just right. (This was not the country, after all.) Then by noon everyone was gone, home for lunch and that cheese. We were "home" for lunch, too, for whatever surprises Tucci had concocted for the day; and after lunch, a *riposo* and then some well-chosen adventure for the afternoon.

We first met Raymond Michel at L'Ermitage when he delivered cheese every morning on his way into town. He has the best cheese in the region, the Tuccis told us, so his shop became a daily destination—sometimes to buy cheese but often just to "shoot the breeze." Raymond, we quickly discovered, was anything but "the little cheesemaker by the lake" as he laughingly described himself. He may not be the tallest Frenchman, but he certainly is one of the liveliest. Driving his red Porsche, climbing high into the Alps for extreme skiing, diving in the Seychelles, Raymond has a sense of adventure that more than matched that of his large American friend.

And like Peter, Raymond is a born iconoclast. One of the favored moments of them both was the annual planning for the cheese we would bring home with us at the end of our trip. A few days before our departure, our morning visit to Raymond's emporium was always devoted to The Great Cheese Discussion. A chair would be produced from the café next door, and Peter would sit down with his five-by-seven cards and the ubiquitous black Flair pen. As cheeses were selected, Raymond would say and Peter would record just how long each would last once we were home—this one to be consumed within a week, others that would last for three weeks, and so on. After they decided on eight or ten cheeses, we departed for our other errands.

The day before we were to leave for home, we picked up the "traveling cheeses," all vacuum-packed by Raymond's sous-vide machine, each with a handwritten note on which Raymond stated "*fromage pasturisé*." Of course most of them were *not* made from pasteurized milk, but this was part of the game Peter and Raymond loved to play. One year we really pushed our luck and bought a whole ham smoked in an Alpine village, knowing that Raymond would vacuum pack it for us. I washed the vacuum-packed ham with soap and water at the hotel, stuffed it into one of Peter's voluminous leather boots, and successfully smuggled it through customs in pre-9/11 New York.

Then one day it was over.

When we arrived at the hotel in the spring of 1992, the Tuccis told us that they'd had an offer for the property. Like everyplace else in the world, it seemed, Annecy was getting richer and fancy people wanted fancy living quarters. The Tuccis had received an offer they couldn't refuse. Chef was tired. Neither of his sons wanted to follow him in the restaurant. So they were considering selling to a developer who wanted their prime lakefront property. We left that year with anxiety, afraid we would never be in that dream world again.

We were right—well, almost. About six months later I came home one day to find Peter shaking his head in both sadness and amusement. "Madame Tucci called," he said. "They have sold L'Ermitage to the developer." With teary eyes I mourned the idea of never sitting on that terrace again, never watching that dining room play unfold. But then Peter recounted the rest of his conversation to me, the part that had him smiling. When he had expressed his distress to Madame Tucci she'd instantly said "*N'inquiete pas*, not to worry. I have picked out the hotel for you all, just the perfect place, in Talloires" (the tiny village further up the lake that she knew we loved). Then she added proudly, "And I have picked out your room! Yes," she explained, "I know the owners well and I went over, picked out the room that is perfect for you, and explained that you always come in the spring or the fall. They should expect you." And sure enough when Peter called Mlle Conan, proprietor of Les Pres du Lac, she said immediately, "Ah, Monsieur Buckley, we are expecting you and Madame Buckley. When are you coming this year? You'll be in room four." And thus began yet another journey into "old France," with personalities and sensibilities and manners that were throwbacks to an earlier age.

So Le Prés du Lac became our headquarters for the annual pilgrimage to France. Gone was the irreplaceable scenario of

L'Ermitage (although we now were invited to the Tuccis' home for fabulous lunches that Chef created just for us, an incredible honor of friendship rarely extended). In its place was a lovely small hotel, with gorgeous lawns that stretched right down to the lake. And another family that, like the Tuccinardis but in a different way, epitomized French tradition in ways fast disappearing. The Conan family had been hoteliers in Talloires since the days when Cézanne came to paint there. The Beau Site was their old traditional lakeside hotel, and Le Prés du Lac was the newer chalet on the property. The Conans were the epitome of old-fashioned hoteliers: gracious, formal, the perfect providers of smooth service—but soon warm friends as well. It was there that we made our new home away from home, loving this new place but always missing the irresistable world of L'Ermitage and dining at Table 2. For if I could choose one place where Peter and I were happiest, one set of memories of Peter, it would be set at Table 2. They're big, full, delicious memories of times when eating with Peter was pure joy.

Gratin Dauphinois à l'Ermitage

We seldom asked Tucci for recipes as they would have been far, far beyond our skills. This one is simple and delicious, however. Of course it's better when the cream and the butter are fresh from the Alps. (Per its French creator, the measurements are metric.)

1 large clove garlic
20 grams of coarse salt plus a pinch, *divided*
Olive oil
¾ liter milk
½–¾ liter cream*
3 eggs (medium or large, not jumbo)
Pepper to taste
¼ tsp. freshly grated nutmeg
1.2 kilos peeled potatoes (russet or other waxy potatoes)
50 grams unsalted butter, diced
50 grams Gruyere, diced

Peel garlic clove and crush with a pinch of coarse salt and a few drops of good olive oil. Rub the entire surface of a flat casserole dish with this paste.

Mix milk and cream with eggs, 20 grams salt, pepper to taste, and nutmeg. Beat this mixture for 7 full minutes. (This breaks up the fibers of the eggs; do not skimp on the time.)

Peel the potatoes and slice very thin using a mandoline. (Tucci says the slices should be "*fine comme une feuille à cigarette*"—as thin as a cigarette paper!) Do not rinse the potatoes. Layer them in the casserole and pour the milk/egg mixture over them. Scatter the diced butter and cheese on top.

Bake for 3 hours at 250°F so the liquid just "smiles." Check the liquid after 3 hours; cook a little longer if the liquid has not been completely absorbed.

*Tucci uses ¾ liter of cream. We felt this left too much liquid, which may be a result of differences in French and American potatoes, size of eggs, or some other factor. We suggest trying it with ½ liter first.

Tucci's Tart Crust

In many decades of making fruit tarts, I have tried recipe after recipe, technique after technique, for making the perfect crust. I adored Tucci's fruit tarts, so he shared this recipe with me one morning as we were leaving Annecy and I was already pining for my tarts. Now, it's my go-to crust recipe.

300 grams butter (the best French butter you can buy), cold, sliced
50 grams sugar
1 egg, beaten
500 grams flour
Salt to taste
Ice water (as needed)

Mix cold sliced butter, sugar, and beaten egg. Cut this mixture into the flour. Add a pinch of salt if you are using unsalted butter.

I pinch some of the pastry together to see if it needs any more moisture. It should hold together smoothly. If it is too dry, add a tablespoon or two of ice water, stirring with a fork. Test again and add a wee bit more water as needed.

Form into three flat circles, like thick pancakes. Wrap in plastic wrap and refrigerate for several hours before rolling out. This recipe makes three crusts. You can freeze the extra for a month or so, and it will still be excellent.

Susan's Blueberry Pie

Happily ceding to Peter all things "dinner," I held forth as the pastry chef. It took much experimenting and the guidance of my Midwestern aunt, but eventually I became the pie queen. Every summer the Greenmarket supplied the fruit for at least one strawberry rhubarb pie, one sour cherry pie, and everyone's favorite, blueberry pie. This is my blueberry pie recipe, with thanks to Elsie Masterton of Blueberry Hill.

Tucci pie crust (see page 174)
1 quart blueberries
¼ cup flour
Scant ½ cup granulated sugar
1 Tbsp lemon juice
Grated rind of 1 lemon
2 Tbsp. brown sugar
1 Tbsp. butter

Roll out one pie crust and line pie plate with it. Place in the freezer while you prepare the blueberries. (This helps make the crust flakier).

In a bowl, mix blueberries, flour, and sugars. Add lemon juice and grated rind. Mix gently but thoroughly, then pour the fruit into the pie plate. Dot with the butter.

Roll out a round of crust to place over the fruit, small enough so that it does not completely cover the top.

Bake in a hot oven at 425°F for 20 minutes, then reduce heat to 375°F and bake until the juice bubbles around the edges of the pie. (To protect the pie edges, you may need to tuck a strip of tin foil around the outside edge of the crust).

For a delicious topping, mix 1 cup of fat free Greek yogurt with 2 Tbsp. heavy cream and a splash of vanilla.

10E AS IN EFFERVESCENT

At home, the daily epicenter of eating with Peter was the big maple table in Apartment 10E—"10E as in effervescent" as Peter always described it. For a quarter of a century, that table was the heart of our family life.

Behind the table hung a large tapestry by Peter's friend, the French artist Jean Lurçat, on it a prancing goat that seemed like a flaming constellation rampant in the sky. It was a perfect image for Peter himself: taking off into flights of fancy, butting heads with everyone, making a little "action" whenever possible—and always dominating the room.

As it had in my Louisiana childhood, dinner occupied an outsized place in the day's events. Planning for dinner, shopping for dinner (at the market and by phone), preparing dinner—for twenty-five years of my life this was Peter's domain. Of course when we got married I thought I should cook half the time, but that foolish idea didn't last very long. In those days I was usually working in an office. Peter was home, and Peter was a way better cook than I. Why in the world should I cook half the time? So pretty soon I stopped. (The end of my cooking came shortly after the first meal I prepared for company, when the entire blender full of watercress soup ended up on the ceiling. What did I know about not putting hot liquid into a blender without letting the steam out?!) I always made desserts, though; I fried chicken (because Lou had taught me how to do that); I set the table; and I put the meal on the table. This last job was a crucial part of the equation, for Peter—who had planned, ordered, and cooked the food—did not want to fix dinner and then sit down to eat it. In his heart he pretended he had a cook who had prepared all of this delicious food, so that he could preside over the table in the lordly manner he wore so easily.

It wasn't just that Peter cooked, however. The key part of this arrangement was that Peter was a fantastic cook, not just a good cook but a *really* skilled cook. He wasn't the sort who took classes or showed off by making tricky creations like soufflés. Nor did he focus on the latest fad, like the American cooks who discovered that green beans did not have to be overcooked but then instead served almost raw beans, which Peter dismissed as "pretentious green beans." No, what he had was a love of good food, a lifetime of exposure to superb cooking, and a deep understanding of flavors. He knew just what spices or vinegars or herbs to add to turn something from good to fabulous. They were what he called "secret ingredients."

Once Peter was going to write a "secret ingredient" cookbook, somehow just the kind of quirky idea that would have amused him greatly. "But you can't do that; then they wouldn't be secret anymore," the children exclaimed, but of course that was just what piqued his provocative sense of humor. Instead, I always wanted Peter to write a book called *Ready Ahead*, for part of his brilliance as a cook was his ability to have a meal ready in advance—all part of that wishing there were a secret cook in the kitchen, preparing his dinners. How did he do it? First of all, he planned everything ahead of time. And then, an early riser, he cooked in the morning, early in the morning, like 5:30 a.m., when there was no one to bother him with conversation or questions. He became an expert in figuring out how to parboil, prep, get everything possible done in advance. And I became an expert at keeping my eyes tightly closed when I woke up, for the moment I opened them, there was action. Somehow Peter would know that I was awake, appear in the doorway, and start the day: "Susan," he would boom, "I have just made a crazy concoction with x, y, and z." Or "Susan, I've already talked to Tucci in Annecy and he says the best way to cook the turnips is like this. . . ." Like so much of life with Peter, it was fascinating and fun, but exhausting.

For many years, part of the secret was the Union Square Greenmarket, where Peter strode from farm stand to farm stand, from friend to friend, planning the coming week's feasts. "Ah, there are gorgeous tomatoes. I'll make gazpacho.

I'll make spaghetti with fresh tomato sauce. I'll make tomato and mozzarella salad—hmmm, that means going to Di Palo's in Little Italy after the market." And on and on. No matter the season, there was food—ingredients—at Union Square that inspired his imagination and his palate.

Every Saturday in the high season—summer and early fall—we bought enough for an army, and that's what it would feed. Peter and I, whatever kids were in residence, plus a parade of dinner guests. Nowadays it seems as though everyone wants to go out, but Peter always preferred home. Cooking was not a chore for him; it was an adventure, an adventure in flavors and combinations, experiments in tastes, and a chance to share all of it with people he loved.

And of course, he was highly skilled at commanding help, arranging our life so that the troops were always at the ready. Saturday mornings, for example: a full index card laid out our itinerary, from Union Square to the Italian grocer Manganaro's to who knows where else, with perhaps a stop at E.A.T. on the way home, to compare notes on cheese with Eli Zabar.

At home, I returned the car to the garage and walked the dog, after Peter had commanding a gaggle of doormen to help empty the car of what seemed like hundreds of bags (we had the world's largest supply of L. L. Bean boat bags). Upstairs, Peter and the bags were met at the door by the unflappable housekeeper, Maria Lumezi. By the time I got home, the two of them were in full swing: cleaning lettuce, cooking those tomatoes, storing the cheeses, preparing the ears of corn we had for dinner every Saturday night in season—all the while discussing the affairs of Maria's large family in Kosovo, the tragedies of Yugoslavia, and the state of the world in general.

Any resident children who might have gone on the Saturday morning outing with us would now have fled the scene entirely, for the Saturday morning rituals at home brought out the most dictatorial side of my beloved husband. As David once observed, Peter could scatter orders like chicken feed. I had my own strategies for dealing with this Saturday morning battle plan, most of which involved preoccupation with the car and the dog in order to avoid the full frontal "military operation" at home. Besides, it was all worth it to me: I didn't have to deal with the food prep and I knew we'd have a delicious dinner on Saturday night. Definitely a win-win situation.

Ninth Avenue was another part of the equation. In the 1970s and 1980s Ninth Avenue was still Hell's Kitchen, filled with Italian butchers and fishmongers and Manganaro's. Actually, there were two Manganaro stores. Ours was the real, original Italian grocery store, founded in 1893 as Manganaro's Grosseriea Italiana. Behind the counter was Sal Dell'Orto, one of the four brothers who had inherited the store. Sal and one brother ran the original store, where the likes of Caruso had shopped when the old Metropolitan Opera was around the corner. After a feud straight out of Puccini, the other two brothers opened Manganaro's Hero Boy next door, selling the enormous six-foot long sandwiches for which they became famous. For us, Manganaro's was a weekly stop on the Saturday marketing caravan. Part of going to Manganaro's was the running conversation and high-drama antics of Sal's wonderful daughters as over the years one by one they came to work in the store, too. Peter loved to tease them and part of every visit was a stream of repartée and laughter, while the ancient

Italian ladies at the counter in the back maintained a constant dialogue in some Italian dialect or other.

Our other classic stop on Ninth Avenue was a visit to Dominick at Central Fish Market, and one day around Easter Dominick convinced Peter that what he really needed to purchase was a live eel. Yes, an eel, a long, slimy, wriggling eel. Dominick would deliver it to the house, he said, and it would be on ice, for cold eels are dormant, quiescent (who knew?). Horrified, I made it clear that I wanted nothing—nada—to do with that eel when it arrived, and Peter assured me that no interaction with said eel would be required. When the package came, Peter quickly put it in the bottom drawer of the refrigerator. Sure enough, the eel didn't move. The next morning, however, it was a different story. When I emerged from the bedroom in a somewhat diaphanous nightgown, Peter suddenly appeared with the eel in his hands. Though it was probably only about a foot long, it looked enormous to me. Recoiling in horror, I backed away, which of course immediately inspired Peter to approach with the eel, wriggling as it began to emerge from its chilled state. Shrieking, I ran to the bathroom and locked the door. I waited. Peter waited. I waited some more. Finally, foolishly assuming that Peter had tired of this game, I opened the door a tiny crack. Wham! Peter and the now very active eel burst into the bathroom. Before I could shriek, however, the eel spied its natural element, water! And before our completely astonished eyes, it slid out of Peter's hands, threw itself into the toilet, and disappeared. It totally disappeared. Remember those stories about alligators in the NYC sewer system? Well, for as long as that eel stayed alive, there really was an eel wandering around down below. Peter and I stood, speechless, for a moment, before we collapsed in laughter. Suffice it to say, we never had a live eel in the house again.

Family dinner was at the heart of every evening. For many years there were assorted children (or the "former children" as Peter called them when they were of a certain nonchildlike age), assorted mothers (Peter's and mine), and assorted friends. Family dinner or company dinner, there was an easy informality about it.

For years I could never eat much for lunch, as I knew that dinner would be something delicious and I'd want to eat lots of it. The helpings were Peteresque in size and so were the plates. We had an Olympic-size collection of plates and bowls of all sizes, mostly from large to larger. For dinner plates, we often used what would be small platters to most people, but Peter deemed them the perfect size so that food wasn't all scrunched together on a too-small plate. They all had geographical names based on where we'd gotten them: the large Canadians, the small Canadians, the large Venetians, the round Venetians, the French reds. And they all have stories. The Venetians, for example: walking by the shop of potter Aldo Rossi in Venice, we spotted gorgeous yellow/umber pottery in the window, went inside, and the next thing we knew Aldo Rossi was designing twelve platters, each with a different fish, twelve round plates each with a different vegetable, twelve large bowls, and twelve small plates to match. A month later it all arrived in crates on our doorstep in New York. Or the Orca plates—really pie plates but just the right shape for a dinner plate when you're having something like stew or a big salad. We had stopped at the pottery on Orca Island in Puget Sound, and loved the color of the plates, which the potter said had been a mistake—everyone adored the turquoise color but he'd never been able to replicate it. We bought all he had.

And then there were the guest books. When *New York Times* reporter Constance Rosenblum did one of her Habitats columns on "10E as in Effervescent," she began with a description of the five guest books "testifying to a life well lived." Over time the guest books, each bound in a different Venetian marbleized paper, took on a life of their own. Often, before they came to dinner, people had heard that one of the requirements was to write in the Buckleys' guest books. You only had to write the first time, but some people were inspired and wrote more than once. The entries are in dozens of languages: English, French, Spanish, and Italian, of course. But also Chinese, and Japanese, and Arabic, and Nahuatl (yes, really), and Thai, and Dutch, and Swedish, and Norwegian, and Akan, and Hawaiian, and Swahili—and probably more that I don't remember. We used to say we'd really be going too far when we invited people to dinner just for the language in which they would write in the guest book (we never did it, I promise).

The guest books open with Peter's as-usual authoritarian instructions: *Please sign your name—and the date—and add a comment. The comment is obligatory, be it tragic, comic, long, or short. You have one page; use it well.* And almost without exception each person wrote on his or her own page (sometimes couples cheated), though sometimes people got carried away and wrote several pages, like Annabel's friend from Venice who created incredibly detailed etchings. "Oh, I can write a story," she exclaimed when presented with the guest book, upon which she promptly disappeared into another room with pen and book in hand. Half an hour later when Peter finally fetched her she had covered pages with spidery, beautiful writing that is almost completely indecipherable, except for the charming beginning: *I have found after much time in a large, cold city, a warm kind evening . . . .*

The tradition of the guest books began in Venice in the summer of 1979. Peter's biography of Ernest Hemingway had just been published, so Peter had brought a set of the unbound pages to one of our favorite Venetian shops, Legattoria Piazzezi. Signora Piazzezi was a tiny, round, charming woman who was highly amused by this eccentric American who towered over her (instead of the usual sobriquet "Salami" as a teasing name, she called Peter "Mortadella," a far larger sausage). When we took the pages to Signora Piazzezi, she and Peter spent a long time picking out just the right gorgeous handmade paper with which she would bind the book. A week later we returned, touched to see that she was so happy with the finished book that she had displayed it in her window. Then she handed us another, small book with blank pages, bound in the same exquisite paper. There was a little paper left over, she explained, and it was far too precious and beautiful to throw away, so she made us this little book. Instantly Peter and I said in unison, "We can have a guest book!" When we got home, Peter inscribed his instructions in the front—enough to intimidate any poor guest, I pointed out to no avail. A week later the first signer was our beloved friend Jane

Kennedy, whom we'd first met in Venice. "*Saluti e mille grazie per la pranzo squisito,*" she wrote. "Greetings and many thanks for an exquisite dinner."

After Margaux Hemingway drew a fabulous, Picasso-esque self-portrait (she took two pages), other people started drawing things, too, so the books are full of self-portraits, sketches of the shells, portraits of the table, pictures of dinner, drawings of the dog in residence.

In the books are pages signed by old friends and new, by children and ancients, and on behalf of dogs who'd come to dinner too. Signed by a gaggle of Hemingways, by the famous bullfighter and by our vet (Peter thought the bullfighter and the vet would get along as each had a special relationship with bulls, but the fact that they shared no mutual language besides bulls put a damper on the conversation), by publishers and writers and violinists and actresses. From the first page in August 1979 to December 1996—the last entry before Peter died—403 dinner guests filled pages with messages long and short. My favorite of all was the ten-year-old who probably had never been out to dinner before and may have been traumatized for life by this unknown requirement of writing after dinner. *I thought it was a nice time*, he carefully wrote. And that said it all. There are pictures and poems and musical scores and song lyrics. There are descriptions of meals, expressions of horror (at being required to do this), and the occasional grouchy note, such as the one from our friend Bill Walton, who detested guest books. Told that the comment was obligatory, his comment was, "*No comment.*"

Not surprisingly, since the task was accomplished after eating dinner, many of the guest book entries describe the food. *You can't be an amateur eater, when you dine with Susan and Peter,* wrote one overstuffed guest. *Of the Buckley pasta, I never get basta,* inscribed another. Leafing through the guest books today I am reminded of how truly delicious Peter's cooking was, and how imaginative and wide-ranging it was. Just like Peter, it was never boring or ordinary. Even the simplest things were wonderful—the perfect ear of corn, perfect roasted potatoes, salad with some exquisite vinegar in the dressing. It always seemed special. And also like Peter, it was sometimes outrageous. One dear friend who grew up in the Midwest eating plain cooking first came to dinner and was served what Peter called "erotic beef"—some kind of beef dish he had concocted with chili peppers and who knows what (it began in his mind as "exotic beef" but was quickly renamed). And the second time the same friend came to dinner, Peter gleefully served octopus salad. It really wasn't that he wanted to test our young friend; it's just that octopus salad was what inspired him that day and he refused to change it when I noted that this might be pushing it a bit for someone who'd undoubtedly never seen an octopus much less eaten one. People should be adventurous, Peter insisted. Indeed, our friend Jamie remembers when she, a blossoming teenager, came to dinner with her parents only to be presented with a whole pig's foot brought to the table on a large platter, surrounded by deliciously steamed vegetables. A pig's foot—she's never forgotten it.

The range of Peter's cooking was immense, inspired by what was in the market or something he'd eaten and loved or some ingredient he read about in the daily *New York Times*. There were phases, too. The gazpacho phase after the trip to

Spain when Peter made one version of gazpacho after another the following summer, as tomatoes overflowed the Greenmarket. Or the risotto phase after a stay in Venice when we'd had particularly fantastic risottos (risotti?) and he interviewed every Italian cook he could about how she (or sometimes he) made their risotto. Or the Bolognese sauce phase after another Italian sojourn. Of course none of us eaters complained, as every version was predictably scrumptious.

Meal after wonderful meal—it's impossible of course to recall them all, but for one brief time I kept a record of my favorites. Tired of always saying to Peter, "Why don't you make that delicious X you made a few weeks ago" and he wouldn't remember just how he'd done it, I decided to write down recipes in a little book. For a short while this project amused Peter no end, and he especially loved making up titles for the dishes. There was one trio of delicious chicken dishes, for example. He called the first Chicken Yes Dear, as that was his response when I said "why don't you make that great chicken with xyz." When he changed it a bit and it was even better, that became Chicken Yes Yes Dear. And—you can imagine the next one—Chicken Yes Yes Yes Dear was the best. Looking through that book brings back such succulent memories and big smiles over dishes like Rabbit Browning and Rat Mouse (ratatouille whipped up into a mousse) and Transcendental Beans, Secret Ingredient Lamb Chops, and Kinky Kidneys (which Peter once served, unthinkingly, to his friend Adrian, a urologist—it was not a success).

For many of these years I was working away from home in one publishing setting or another. In those days before email and smartphones, once I was home, work was over, and I was always home in time for Peter and me and whoever else was there—children and/or guests—to sit down for drinks before dinner. Drinks and talk, a flow of ideas sped along by Peter's buoyant curiosity and fervent imagination. The headmaster of Michael's school summed it up perfectly when he began his guest book page with *The Pope of the Lexington Avenue Vatican sits/And edits the world in a series of fits.* Such a perfect, teasing evocation of "the autocrat of the dinner table." It wasn't that Peter dominated the conversation by talking all the time, not at all, but he somehow guided it always toward some subject that interested him. And he always had strong opinions to voice.

This all seemed perfectly normal to me. After all, at my grandparents' table in Louisiana from a very young age you were expected to have opinions and to voice them—politely but articulately. Certainly at the Louisiana dinner table, we never played "the desert island game," however. I don't know where the game came from—probably from the English radio program, Desert Island Disk, on which a celebrity chose his or her favorite record—but it was one of the Buckley dinner table capers forever. Out of the blue, someone—usually one of the kids—would say "okay" in a certain cadence and everyone would await the coming puzzle: If you could have only one on a desert island, would you choose meat or fish? If you could have only three cheeses, what would they be? What nationality would you choose? What friend would you take? And on and on. We played it with an intensity that amazes and amuses me now, and it always involved pointed discussions and often some incredulity: Would you really choose only *brie??* Why would you want an Italian rather than a French companion? Hmmm. The discussions were half the fun.

What possesses a respectable couple of world travelers on the Upper East Side to invite eternally grateful people to fine dinners with finer chatter, wrote our friend who had survived both erotic beef and octopus salad. What possessed both Peter and me was a great love for friends, food, and conversation. *A celebration—a feast, Christmas, and birthdays—all rolled into one glorious, greedy, happy evening,* wrote one contented dinner guest years earlier. And so they were, those dinners at the maple table in 10E.

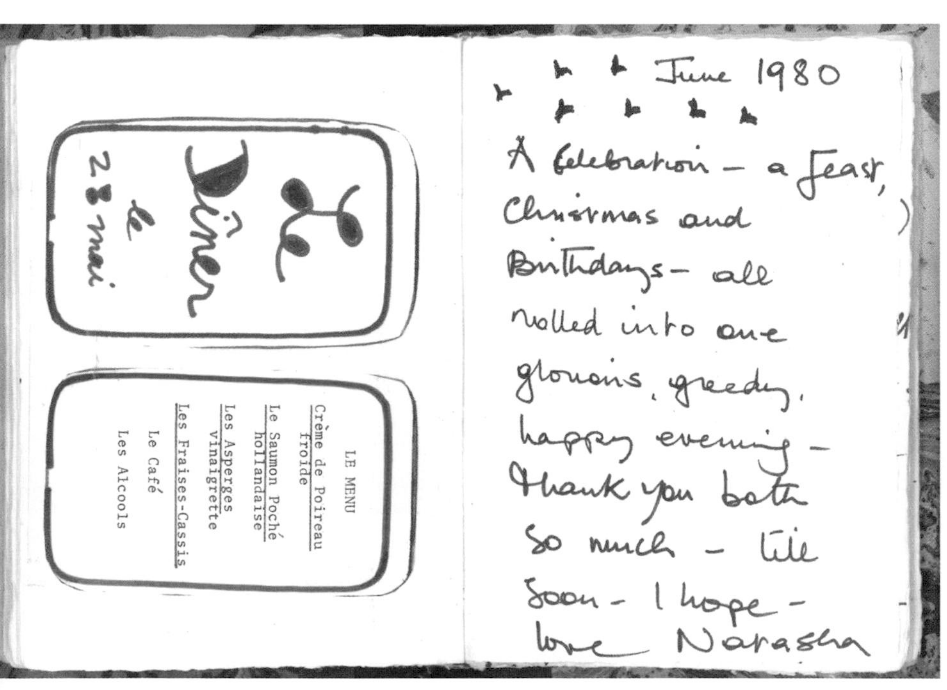

Le Dîner
le 28 mai
LE MENU
Crème de Poireau froide
Le Saumon Poché hollandaise
Les Asperges Vinaigrette
Les Fraises-Cassis
Le Café
Les Alcools
June 1980
A Celebration – a feast,
Christmas and
Birthdays – all
rolled into one
glorious, greedy,
happy evening –
Thank you both
so much – till
soon – I hope –
love Natasha

Watercress Soup

Peter's version of the soup I blendered onto the kitchen ceiling.

- 4 cups homemade chicken broth
- 7 small white onions
- 6-8 large cloves of garlic, sliced
- 1 bay leaf
- 3-4 bunches of watercress, well cleaned
- 1 cup buttermilk
- ½ cup heavy cream

Make homemade chicken broth with only chicken and water. Remove bones and skin, and degrease, but do not strain broth.

In 4 cups of chicken broth, cook white onions and garlic. Add bay leaf. Boil just till soft.

Add well-cleaned watercress. Cook 1–2 minutes after watercress has wilted. Remove bay leaf. Add buttermilk.

COOL MIXTURE before putting in blender or food processor, so it doesn't end up on the ceiling!!!!!!!! Then blend thoroughly.

Before serving, add heavy cream in desired amount. (When I make this today, I add buttermilk to the soup mixture, then add a tablespoon of cream in each bowl.)

Chicken Yes Yes Yes Dear

One of the Yes Dear trilogy of chicken recipes.

4 medium to large bell peppers (preferably 1 each: red, yellow, orange, green)
3 red onions (baseball-size)
½ cup olive oil
½ cup red wine vinegar
¼ tsp. cayenne pepper
Salt and pepper to taste
12-oz. package of thick-sliced bacon or slab bacon, diced
⅓ cup chopped fresh sage
1 cup dry red wine (such as Côte du Rhone)
12 chicken thighs (skin on, bone in)
3 chicken livers

Note: Reserve and use all fat (olive oil, chicken, bacon) as you cook.

Cut peppers into roughly 16 full-length slices. Chop onions roughly. Brown peppers and onions in olive oil in a large Dutch oven. Add ½ cup vinegar and ¼ tsp. cayenne to the vegetables.

Sprinkle chicken thighs with salt and pepper, then sauté to golden brown. Remove to a large bowl.

Frizzle the diced bacon, rendering most of the fat. (Peter boiled the bacon ahead of time till soft, to reduce the amount of fat.) Don't let the bacon get too crisp, however. Add ⅓ cup chopped fresh sage to bacon in the last 2 minutes of cooking. Add all (including bacon drippings) to the vegetables.

Add 1 cup red wine, then nestle the chicken thighs in the vegetable "goo." If desired, add 3 chicken livers, which you have lightly sautéed, or serve the livers separately.

Simmer at low heat for 30 minutes or until done, adjusting the thighs during cooking as needed. Add a little more red wine if needed.

Remove from heat and let rest for 2–3 hours. Reheat at medium heat 15 minutes before serving.

Daube

Peter loved to read recipes, but then he would make them his own—like this, from Marcel Pagnol's Favorite Recipes from Provence, *by Jacqueline Pagnol.*

POULTRY

QUAIL IN COCOTTE

Ingredients:
2 quails per person,
juniper berries,
fresh thyme,
salt, pepper,
1 slice of bacon per quail,
10 cloves of garlic,
1 bottle of dry white wine.

Serves 6 to 8.

Stuff the quails with juniper berries, salt and pepper. Wrap them with a slice of bacon, each held on with a tooth pick.

Saute in the cocotte* with fresh thyme, 10 cloves of garlic in their skin, and pour the white wine on, approximately 20 minutes before the end of the cooking.

Serve on toast soaked in the gravy. You can spread some foie gras on them and serve with baked potatoes.

Drink a light red wine with it.

* A cocotte is a heavy pot made of fireproof earthenware or cast iron.

MEAT

2 Days

DAUBE

DAUBE

Ingredients:
2 cups of wine (white or red)
3 pounds of stewing beef of different kinds like " La Galinette" which is the top of the leg muscle, the cheek which is a very tender part, and
at least 1 or 2 other boneless stewing meats. 1 calf's foot
4 cloves of garlic,
bay leaf, fresh thyme,
parsley, 4 large onions,
orange peel, salt, peppercorns,
1/2 cup olive oil,
1/2 cup wine vinegar.

Serves 6 to 8 persons.

for 7

The day before, I marinate the cubes of different kinds of meat with the crushed garlic, the orange peel, salt, peppercorns, olive oil and wine vinegar.

The next day, in an earthenware cocotte (casserole), I saute the onions slowly and remove them when golden. Then I add the chunks of meat, stirring well. I mix the marinade and the onions. When everything is brown, I pour in one cup of hot water, cover, simmer for 4 hours on very low flame. At the end, you must add a good glass of white wine (or red as you wish).

One eats it with wide Italian pasta or polenta.
During the summer, the Daube can also be served cold with its jelly.

eat with POLENTA

Drink a light Bordeaux.

2 cups Red Wine
3 lbs. Beef
1 Cow Foot
4 garlic cloves
Salt
peppercorns
4 Big Onions
Bay
Thyme
Orange Peel
1/2 cup Oil
1/2 cup Vinegar

MEAT

ROUGAIL OF SAUSAGE
SAUSAGE ROUGAIL

Ingredients:
3 chopped onions,
8 chopped tomatoes,
6 large sausages,
4 hot red small peppers,
minced garlic, olive oil,
chive,
2 cans of red kidney beans.

Serves 6 to 8 persons.

Spread the olive oil in a skillet large enough so that all the ingredients can be mixed. Saute onions, tomatoes, garlic and red peppers. Add the sliced sausages. Stir for a few minutes until sausages are golden. Lower the heat and simmer for 10 minutes. Add the red beans, wait another 10 minutes. Sprinkle with chive before serving.

Drink a light red Cote du Rhone.

10

Afterwards

Peter died on January 8, 1997.

The last few years of Peter's life were hard for everyone, as he struggled with complications from diabetes. At one point I opined that this was once a wonderful man who was sometimes impossible, but now was an impossible man who was sometimes wonderful.

Somehow, it seemed as though his larger-than-life personality would endure forever. Then one day he was gone. Corporeally, that is. For weeks his spirit hovered in every cranny of the apartment, when I went to the farmers' market, when I was in the park. "You didn't really think Peter was going to *leave*, did you?" our friend Elspeth asked.

Ten years earlier, Peter's mother had died. She had demanded, adamantly, that there be no service and that her ashes be distributed in the Atlantic by Frank Campbell's, the venerable Upper East Side dispatcher of the no-longer-living. The children and I were horrified by what felt to us like such a cold ending to one's life.

So, the fall after Elinor entered the Atlantic, when Peter and I were sitting on the terrace at L'Ermitage, overlooking our beloved Lake Annecy, I said to him, "Assuming I outlive you, I want to have my ashes wherever yours are, and I have no intention of having Campbell's scatter me in the frigid waters of the North Atlantic! So where do you want your ashes to go?"

"Well, my passport is American, but my soul is French," Peter said, as he'd oft observed in the past. "I want to be right here in this lake, near all of these places I love." So, when the time came, I knew what to do.

The first step was transporting Peter's ashes and the family to France. Getting the ashes to France was not a simple proposition, it turned out. French bureaucracy had, as bureaucracies are wont to do, created a Cartesian list of requirements that included the urn being enclosed in a bronze container, which then had to be taken to the French consulate where it was inspected, approved, and finally sealed shut with gold wire and red sealing wax stamped with the figure of Marianne. Accompanied by an awe-inspiring sheaf of official papers, Peter's earthly remains were brought back to me by Frank Campbell's. He would have loved the pomp and circumstance, we all agreed, especially the elegant red sealing wax.

Finally on a beautiful Sunday morning in June, we all found ourselves in a boat on Lake Annecy. Of course it's illegal to scatter ashes in the lake, but people do it all the time. I had approached the "boat family" in Talloires, whom we'd known for years, and their son said he would be honored to take us out on the lake. He just rolled his eyes when I asked if anyone would give us trouble about the ashes.

We scattered Peter's ashes on the lake by the castle Cézanne once painted. At one end of the lake, the Alps stood out sharply against a perfect blue sky. At the other end was the canal-laced old town of Annecy. It was a place Peter loved more than anywhere else on Earth. And every time I go back, it seems perfect to imagine him floating around in the lake, in the clouds, above the mountains—supervising life on Lake Annecy.

Afterward we went to church in the tiny village chapel in Menthon-Saint-Bernard, where the priest spoke of Peter as "*un grand ami de la région.*" And then we had a luncheon for the close friends we had made around the lake over the years. In addition to us, there were our antiquarian friends Assunta and Jacques Chatelain; the Tuccis of course; Dr. Casez, Peter's beloved French doctor; Raymond Michel with his wife, Jeannine; and Mlle Conan, in whose charming inn we now stayed.

I had planned the lunch with Monsieur Conan, who still ran the perfect old-fashioned hotel where we had eaten so many times, overlooking the lake. As I sat with him in the garden, just after we arrived from New York, I felt as though Peter was smiling down on me, so proud of all the lessons I had learned. I could discuss in French just what fish we should have and how it should be prepared, which local wine would be perfect for a summer luncheon, and which berries were the best for dessert at this time of year. Monsieur Conan smiled at me and observed that he was certain Monsieur Buckley would approve of our choices.

We spent a bittersweet week along Lake Annecy, then I headed south with Annabel, her husband, Ben, and their young son, Lorenzo. We had one more mission.

When Peter died, I had telephoned our friends in France with the news. In a tiny village near Arles were our friends, the proprietors of a beloved auberge where we had often stayed. They asked about the disposition of Peter's ashes. "Please," they said, "save a little bit of Peter for the rose garden." Annabel and I agreed that the rose garden would be the perfect spot for the urn that still contained a residue of Peter in its bronze magnificence.

When we arrived at the auberge, everything was ready. Our friends had collected dried roses for us, and we filled the urn with the petals. The Portuguese porter at the hotel had been a stonemason in his youth, and he had prepared a niche in the centuries-old wall that surrounded the garden. Annabel and I placed the rose-filled urn in the niche, said our good-byes to Peter, and then the urn was enclosed within the wall. The porter carefully carved PHB and a cross into the wall in front of the niche. And for the next decade or more, Peter inhabited the garden as well as Lake Annecy.

A few years ago, however, our friends decided that it was time to retire. They sold the hotel and retreated to their house in the village (the French word for "retirement" being a retreat). I was sad on many levels, knowing that I would never again be able to sit in that rose garden or dine in the exquisite barrel-ceilinged dining room where olive oil was once stored or listen to the maître d'hôtel explain the intricacies of the Provençal language. But I also was alarmed about what might happen to the rose garden.

Sure enough, the website of the new hotel soon showed a large swimming pool where the garden once bloomed. What about the wall? What about Peter's urn? I fretted. I knew that our friends were distressed though philosophical about the changes, and I was hesitant to ask about Peter's whereabouts. But I needn't have worried.

Recently, the daughter of the house came to visit me in New York.

"What about Peter's ashes?" I asked.

"Oh," she said, "Peter lives with us now!"

"What do you mean?" I exclaimed.

She explained. When her father realized what was happening to the rose garden, he decided to take action. On a moonless night, he crept into the remains of the garden, removed Peter's urn from the wall, and took it home.

"Peter is up in my old room," the daughter explained. "He has a wonderful view of the village and the windmill. Yes, Peter lives with us now," she said with a happy smile.

Ah Peter, you always did know how to find yourself in the best spot of all.

After Peter died, in January 1997, I don't think I ate for months. I did, of course, but nothing tasted right and I certainly wasn't having dinner parties. But then little by little I emerged, and as I did, I realized that having friends for dinner was such an integral part of my life that I couldn't, shouldn't, wouldn't give it up. I'll never forget the first company for dinner, lifelong friends from Louisiana who would love me no matter what I put on the table. But I was in a state of panic. There was no Peter to plan and cook the dinner with exuberance and panache. There was no one to go to the market with or to engage the butcher in a spirited discussion on cuts of meat. There was no one, I remember wailing to myself. But I did it, and it was fine.

Pretty soon I realized that I had absorbed all kinds of lessons from my years of eating with Peter. I knew how to find the best ingredients, how to put together a menu, how to be "ready ahead" so that I could enjoy my guests. Of course I had to make adjustments. Without Peter's incredible internal clock, for example, I developed what I call "the Pavlovian school of cooking," lots of timers ringing so that I don't get so lost in a conversation that I forget what is happening in the kitchen. I knew we were in a different era, though, when a new friend, complimenting me on dinner asked innocently, "Oh, was Peter a good cook, too?" Yes, Chris, he was a very good cook indeed.

The guest books and I have moved to a new apartment, where dinner parties continue and the Lurçat tapestry still hangs by my dinner table—and the spirit of Peter keeps an eye on things, ready to make a little action in case anyone is bored, ready to be outrageous when needed.

Acknowledgments

Over the years that I've been writing these stories, I owe my first and largest debt to my Writer's Group: to Dana Catharine, who is the real midwife of these stories (as well as their superb and loving illustrator), and to Sunita Apte, Malcolm Farley, and now James Kemp.

My deepest gratitude and affection to my publisher, the incomparable Jeannette Seaver, for loving these stories and wanting to publish them. To my friend Will Schwalbe, who believed in this book and suggested that I show it to Jeannette. To Charlotte Sheedy for giving me a "mitzvah." And to everyone at Arcade, for turning these stories into a real book.

Thanks to David and Annabel for keeping me honest. And to the gentle ghosts who were once part of these tales: to much loved Michael Buckley, always missed; to my wonderful mother, Lora French Ruess, who set me on the path to adventure; and to my mother-in law, Elinor Buckley, who taught me the difference between being a tourist and a traveler.

To four friends who gave me their professional advice and the confidence that this could be a published work: Maggie Simmons, Beth Gutcheon, Moira Hodgson, and Stephen Schmidt.

To my valiant recipe contributors and testers: Steven Lipsitz, Sue Hamilton, Annabel Wildrick, David Buckley, Francoise Firmin, and Maurice Tuccinardi.

And to all of the dear friends who read these stories and urged me on over the years: Steve Lipsitz for his wise edits, as well as Beth and David Carpenter, Linda Beech, Dottie and Peter Brooke, Marcia Cantarella, Kevin Colleary, Abby Conklin, Philip Conklin and Philippa Kirby, Terry Cooper, Margarita Danielian, Chris Hegedus and D. A. Pennebaker, Carollyne Hutter, Lois Kauffman, Elspeth Leacock, Phyllis Levin, Elena Mannes, Pamela McCorduck, Patrick Meade, Molly and Norman McGrath, Danny Miller, Margot Nadien, Barbara Richert (with special thanks for French sleuthing), Lynne Rutkin and Raymond Liddell, Patricia Santelli and David Hamilton, Marcia Schonzeit, Patricia Soussloff, Wendy Stein, Jodie Ulmer, and Susan Whittlesey.